As I have traveled all over the world, I have seen such devastation in the hearts and lives of so many people. It has been a wonderful experience to see so many of them healed. In *Fragments to Freedom*, Joy shares some of the hell that she went through... not stayed in! She is so willing to share what happened to her and she received *complete* freedom through Jesus Christ. We are an example of what God can do if we just give our broken and abused hearts to Him. I encourage everyone to read this book and get completely free.

—Joan Hunter
Founder and President of Joan Hunter Ministries
Author of *Healing the Heart* and many other books

FRAGMENTS
to Freedom

FRAGMENTS
to Freedom

Healing from
Dissociative
Identity
Disorder

M. JOY KAIROS

W. WinePressPublishing
Great Books, Defined.

WinePress Publishing (PO Box 428, Enumclaw, WA 98022) functions only as book publisher. As such, the ultimate design, content, editorial accuracy, and views expressed or implied in this work are those of the author.

ISBN 13: 978-1-4141-1846-8
ISBN 10: 1-4141-1846-5
Library of Congress Catalog Card Number: 2010908188

To my adopted family

Snoopy, Auntie, Meritail, Mitten, and AppleDoc: you became the first place my heart could call home. You gave me a home of love and rest, where I could begin to heal and become alive again. The year living in your home will never be forgotten for any of us. No matter where we are in the world, I know my heart can be safe at home again because of your love for me.

Contents

—⁂⁂○—

Acknowledgments

NUMEROUS PEOPLE HAVE walked with me in my journey from fragmentation to freedom. Each was a treasure of His truth. I have found jewels of Him within them. I can't help but mention a few significant in my journey.

Michelle: from the beginning of my healing, you have been a friend as consistent as the sunrise to remind me the Son rose and came to set me free.

Kathy: I will never forget your encouragement to break away from all darkness. I finally broke away. I'm not satisfied being whole all by myself; now I must tell others about Him.

Alaine: I watched you for years, and I saw your hunger for His Word. You taught me that the God of the Scriptures was on my side by your insatiable appetite for Him.

Jossie: you had me promise never to give up pursuing healing and freedom. You knew I would know freedom even when neither of us knew how or when it would come.

Brent: you provided a safe place to cry when life seemed too much. You let me discover I didn't have to be silent anymore. You were one of the first safe men in my life. You never told me what Christ is like, but lived what Christ is like.

Pastor Risa: you showed me how to live in the secret place of the Lord, where the enemy can't find me. You taught me where my heart can war and rest in Him alone.

Pastors David and DeeDee: you were the first pastors who showed me it was safe to cry, process, question, laugh, dance, and worship. You gave permission for my perspectives of who God was to be transformed in my life as He healed me. You had every reason to cease walking with me on numerous occasions, but you didn't. You kept interceding and allowed me to discover who He is. When I first heard of you two, the comment was, "I would trust any life pursuing healing and wholeness into their hands." They were not mistaken. Thank you for investing your lives in me. Your willingness to minister to those with SRA/DID and walk with me until I crossed the finish line of freedom isn't found among many.

I am grabbing the baton and continuing to run for those after me, pursuing healing and freedom. Let us run for joy for all He has for us as part of His Kingdom Church ministering to those broken and captive.

Except for these acknowledgments, all names in the book have been changed.

A special thank you to:

Beverly—for help with the "jots" and "tittles."

The intercessory prayer team—without your labor in prayer these pages wouldn't have been. I praise God for each of you as you encouraged and prayed me through this process.

DID/SRA 101

DISSOCIATIVE IDENTITY DISORDER (DID), formally known as Multiple Personality Disorder (MPD) and Satanic Ritual Abuse (SRA) are often associated with various terms not commonly used outside of a psychological domain. Some of these terms are listed below in addition to characteristics of a person with DID/SRA. These are mentioned to give a foundation for understanding DID/SRA as you read a journey of healing from abuse and brokenness pertaining to dissociation caused by abuse in satanic rituals.

Dissociative Identity Disorder (DID) is a psychological disorder indicating a person's mind has experienced trauma so severe a part of the person's mind "splits" into another "personality" so the person herself (or himself) does not have to carry the pain. Instead, this personality, or "part" or "alter," carries the pain of the experience/memory, whereas the person herself is amnesic to the trauma that occurred.

Dissociation—a form of separation from reality a person experiences; there are various forms of dissociation. DID is dissociation to an extreme, as the person is not aware of the events that she lives in while she has dissociated. An "alter" or another "personality" lives through her during the dissociated state of mind. There's a separation between what the person lives and what the alter lives while the person isn't aware. As healing happens, this separation merges.

Alter/Part/Personality—a dissociated part of the person's mind/core personality. An alter speaks from the age from when her trauma occurred. For example, if the trauma occurred when she was five, the alter will have a five-year-old voice and the personality of a five-year-old. The number of alters or personalities inside a dissociated mind can be as few as one other, to hundreds, depending on the severity of trauma experienced.

Integration—merging of alters/parts/personalities to come into wholeness of the core person's mind and emotions. Complete integration is when the person no longer hears the alters' voices and has complete memories of trauma the alters carried.

Memories—when associated with DID/SRA, alters often carry memories filled with horror related to satanic abuse, rituals, and ceremonies. They are often vowed to be kept secret, but the Lord can expose and heal them all.

Voices—there are three main kinds of voices one with DID/SRA hears constantly inside his or her mind. All are heard internally, inside the person's mind. The first kind are voices of the personalities constantly talking internally. They talk with each other, to the person, and to demonic voices inside the person's mind.

Demonic voices are the second kind of voice the person hears all the time. They are not always distinguished immediately between the various personalities/alters. These demonic voices can pose as alters to confuse healing. This is one reason why the gift of discernment of spirits and knowing how to hear from the Lord are also important.

The third voice is the voice of the Lord, one voice. The person can hear the voice of the Lord as the Lord always speaks. The challenge is that the person often isn't aware of God's voice because so many others are speaking at the same time. The demonic voices also speak directly against the voice of the Lord, causing confusion for the person to believe he or she has heard the voice of the Lord.

Losing Time—the time an alter/personality/part is living the person's life as her personality's age while the core person herself is not aware of what is happening or what she is doing, technically known as an "amnesic state," while the personality is "out."

Characteristics of people with DID (used by permission from Lydia Discipleship Ministries):

1. Socially inappropriate
    *   They often withdraw from crowds or even people trying to befriend them.
    *   They may respond to various situations with immature reactions.
    *   They have difficulty with close relationships—suspicion, jealousy, and misunderstanding.
    *   They may have limited communication skills.
    *   They often have a caustic "protector personality" who is used in responding to threats with intense self-protection.
    *   They tend to take things personally.
    *   They don't share likes and dislikes or what they want to do because it's always changing. It's hard to make friends with them.
    *   They are people pleasers who find it hard to be totally honest.

- They often shade the truth if they don't think it will be well received.
- Often they are insecure.
- They can't handle another's anger or even mild displeasure toward them.
- They try to read the other person's mind and how the person will respond before they give their opinion.

2. Intense Self-Hatred
   - They may self-abuse (i.e., cutting/slashing face, arms, pulling out hair, clawing skin, etc.). They may punish themselves inside with disgust or loathing of self, fueled by the demonic, murderous hatred.
   - Cutting can also serve as a pain releaser; the level of anguish inside is so great that slashing with a razor blade is miniscule in comparison. Self-abuse is definitely *not* intended as an attention getter.
   - They may make suicide attempts.
   - They have very high expectations of demands on themselves that often drive them into worka-holism.
   - Sometimes after failure, they self-abuse, thinking, "I should be past this already and able to do the right thing." They have little grace for themselves and therefore for others.

3. Identity Crises
   - If they are aware of the different parts inside, they see them as individual people who are part of them and often will know the names.
   - May believe that they are not a person, not a human being.
   - They don't believe they have the right to say no.
   - They have no sense of anything belonging to them.

- They see themselves as either overly sexual or nonsexual beings.
- They have a profound ambivalence about their relationship with God. They are mad at God for allowing their abuse, yet they desire to draw close to Him. They feel rejected by God.
- They are very afraid to trust God or anyone else who extends kindness to them.

4. Loneliness
   - This is often a self-fulfilling prophecy. They believe, "If they really get to know me, they will reject me," and unconsciously try to prove that the person will eventually give up on them as all others have.
   - They have a great desire for secrecy. Often this comes from a pattern of threats from the past to not tell.
   - They have a pervasive sense of vulnerability.

5. Demonic Presence
   - They may hear voices, blasphemy, threats, or blackmail attempts in their head.
   - They may face outside (not from within their minds) cult threats.
   - The demons may make it impossible to read Scripture by putting the individuals to sleep when they read or pray.
   - They have an intense feeling that they have to run, to escape.
   - They may know truth in their heads, but their intense emotional responses keep them from acting on that truth.

6. Inability to be Involved in Church Events, Ceremonies
    - Communion is very difficult because of the symbolism as well as the demonic interference.
    - They usually have trouble sitting through sermons because of the use of Scripture as well as other triggers.
    - Even in a crowd, they feel like outsiders, or a "space alien."

7. Problems with Their Minds
    - They have difficulty staying in reality due to distractions of "mind noise."
    - They have an inability to focus for long periods of time.
    - They may jump from one topic to another.
    - They often experience severe mood swings as another alter gets "strong."
    - Largely due to demonic interference, they can't remember or read Scripture.

8. Feeling Violated and Under the Control of Others
    - They may have a strong desire to keep as much of their lives as possible under their control.
    - Feeling out of control may be reflected in how they keep their immediate environment (home, work space, etc.).
    - They allow sexual intimacy only when they say and how they say based on their intense fear of losing control of the situation.
    - Some may lack the ability to be intimate because if they are, they are breaking a promise to themselves that no one will be able to arouse them again.

9. Feeling Vulnerable and Helpless
   - Medical tests and hospitalization may feel like abuse.
   - Going under anesthesia may feel the same as losing control again.
   - Having to undress, either in front of a male or female, causes shame, terror, and feelings of helplessness.

Introduction

—⁂—

MY SOUL HAD many voices inside. God came and heard them. My mind was a plethora of personalities. God came and gathered them. He healed their hurts. He made them one whole, healed mind. This book tells the journey of my life during the chaos of being crushed in spirit. It tells how my mind split into personalities. This book exposes schemes of the enemy associated with Satanic Ritual Abuse (SRA) that I experienced, causing me to have Dissociative Identity Disorder (DID). Different split personalities inside my mind are also called "alters," "voices in my head," "ones inside," or "parts." To help prevent confusion I will refer to them throughout this book as alters. These pages proclaim the power and mercy of the Lord to rescue me from my life of torment and SRA. I will give glimpses into my mind before healing happened.

Before healing happened, alters who were in my mind constantly talked, yelled, cried, screamed, journaled, argued, and talked more. Throughout this book various journal entries and phrases of what they said are written from their voice to help give perspective of what my mind was like before the Lord healed me. Before I explain how my mind became whole again from the horror I will talk about their perspectives during various points in the healing process. Their "voices" will be in a different font.

Internal confusion and chaos I experienced, how the Lord healed memories, and steps of healing from DID/SRA will be discussed. My mind once fragmented is now integrated and free from fear, horror, torment, and chaos. Strongholds that captivated me are also exposed as fortresses of truth in those areas continue to be built. I will talk about different resources the Lord used to help me heal and understand spiritual warfare. As He taught me who I am in Him, and set me in a family, the journey of healing develops in the meantime of integration. Later, as He brought me to a crossroads to freedom, I learn what normalcy is and discover how drastically different my life is without darkness.

To one who doesn't yet understand me, I may sound like I am talking in a different language. I may not make sense to people who don't know about alters inside someone's mind. I used to believe I was crazy. God saw everything. He transformed my mind. I know other people may not believe me yet. Keep reading. The Lord rescued me, because He delighted in me. He calls me His beloved, His daughter, healed and whole in Him. He saw my future mind and soul before I began to see my own devastation of being shattered inside.

The pictures I saw weren't normal. The voices I heard inside my mind were unusual. I was afraid to speak of what happened behind my eyes. I feared that if I told, no one would understand. I didn't know what would happen if I got brave and spoke.

What is it like for someone to understand or hear me? I imagined what would happen if I found someone who believed me and could help. I waited as one drowning, not knowing how to swim, for the lifeguard to see me and jump in after me. I wanted them to embrace me and bring me to the surface, where I could live again. Emotions and pictures splattered my canvas soul. I lived in darkness, as voices of death, destruction, and terror were my best friends. I didn't know if there was hope for me. What could I say to someone who wanted to help me? What if I didn't make sense? All I could do was hope someone could help in the midst of my mental mysteries and scattered soul. This book declares the deliverance that found me: Jesus Christ of Nazareth. He did come, hear, understand, and heal me.

When I was five years old and the SRA was occurring most nights of my life, I knew my name was written in the goat's book of death. This is the book where names are listed for those who walk in darkness and follow Satan. I remember when my name was written in blood in the goat's book of death. I didn't know if I was supposed to be excited my name was in the book or afraid of what they would require of me. Then I had a dream. This dream is when I first heard of who God is and about the true Lord Jesus Christ. Every other idea I had of Him was based on what happened in satanic ceremonies, where He was severely mocked. This brought confusion in me as to who He really was. In the dream I was in heaven, sitting on Jesus' lap while He read to me the names in the Lamb's book of life. He knew I loved books and reading even then. It was safe on His lap. He kept flipping pages so large filled with thousands of names. I asked Him, "How do you get your name in this book?" This one, compared to the book of death I knew, was full of light and names written as though they were cared for. He replied, "All you have to do is love Me." I never have forgotten replying, "I want to love You instead." As soon as I said that He brought out His special pen and wrote down a name. I said, "That's not my name." He said, "It is not your name now, but it will be. I write down the name I have named you." I was content with the name He gave me and that my name was now written in the Lamb's book of life. I awoke from my dream and wondered if there was a book called the Lamb's book of life.

Later I discovered in Scripture the Lamb's book of life and knew at that point the Lord had His hand on my life in a unique way. Even when all the darkness continued to take place He had a way for me to escape and know Him for who He is. I am often asked, "When was it you came to know the Lord?" I always think about that dream and wonder if it was then, even though I was forced and then chose to participate in the satanic ceremonies, or if it was many years later in college when I chose to break away from the darkness I was walking in. It was this time in college I chose to give my heart to the Lord the best way I knew how. However, I was still involved with much darkness because alters inside were actively involved while I was unaware. In college, because I also attended church on Sundays most weeks of my life, yet simultaneously participated in darkness, I had severe distortions of who God is.

Confusion and memories began to surface during this time, my senior year in college after my father died. I talked with someone about wanting to follow the Lord shortly after my father died. I was afraid. I knew I wanted to be free. I wanted to keep my secrets. Memories were leaking into my day life and tormented me. I wanted the horror to be gone. I wanted to keep the control and power I thought I had. I wanted to be normal. I still wanted to die. I wanted a quiet mind. I wanted life. I wanted to go away forever and be forgotten. I wanted life and hope. I didn't know how to get there. This was only the beginning.

Perhaps it would be helpful to give some hints as to what goes on within one who is healing from DID/SRA. As alters explain hints of my horror, it may help to relate to you, the reader, what they are saying. Scenarios or memories described may give insight and understanding to the healing process. I hope to give greater understanding for helpers if they encounter similar situations. This book is intended for those healing from DID/SRA and for those who desire to help. My heart is for the hurting and the helper to be encouraged. Tools I have discovered to help persevere during this journey of healing and freedom are also shared.

Among these pages I pray you will find the God of hope. Maybe you are reading as one who is hurting inside, hoping someone may understand what you constantly face. Maybe you are a helper desiring to come alongside a hurting person, with greater understanding for what's happening in them. However you come, my desire is for you to walk away from these pages with an increased love for the One who rescues us from the miry clay and sets our feet upon His Rock.

I hope to portray to those hurting there is hope. The truth does set us free, and they are not alone in their struggles to survive. I hope to give inside peeks of what life could be like on a road leading to healing and freedom. A life of freedom is possible. Healing and freedom come in Jesus Christ alone. To the helper of those hurting I hope to give clarity of what may be going on inside a hurting person with DID/SRA as he or she courageously journeys to find life. I hope to give insight to some issues happening inside the mind of one with DID/SRA.

Some portions of this book are written from one who is hurting, and various journal entries will expose the reality of what they experienced. Other portions are written from a helper's perspective. They will talk about when they came alongside and how they learned how to help the hurting person. They tell how they discovered the Pandora's box of pain that lay dormant inside. They will share how their prayer life increased and how their perspective of the Lord changed. These pages are also practical tools helpers can use as they learn to walk together in places of healing and freedom.

My prayer is that you will discover the gracious heart and the intense passion of the Lord to come, restore, and heal us. He longs to bring us from a place of being shattered inside to a place of uncompromised wholeness and transformation. I pray you will come to know Jesus Christ in ways you have never known Him before. The One who merges slivers of shattered glass in hearts and minds and creates them into majestic mosaics of stained glass wants to do the same for you. I pray you will see His glory revealed when others walk by in awe of an illustrious act of the Lord. I pray you will come to know a God who takes the fragments of a mind with Dissociative Identity Disorder and takes such gentle care of each significant alter. In His impeccable timing, He places them in their destined places where no one else could have fit. He brings order from chaos as He puts pieces of a mind's puzzle together again.

I pray that in the process and timing of it all, you will know Jesus Christ, who is not unaware of the torment and pain when it may seem He didn't come in time. I pray you discover a God who is keenly aware. He knows the story and absolute timing for freedom in each one. He never leaves one behind. I pray you will see how He knows all aspects of emotional healing needing to take place and how He never rushes or overwhelms. He knows we are but dust.

I'm asking the God of all hope to fill your mind and heart through Christ Jesus. God wants more than anything for us to have greater understanding of His love for us. He wants us to be free even more than our yearnings for freedom. It is for freedom Christ has come. I'm asking our Savior to help me explain what life was like before healing from DID/SRA for those who want to help. I will expose portions of my own journey of healing from Dissociative Identity Disorder and Satanic Ritual Abuse. Trauma and dances of *tehilah* accompanied my trails in the wilderness. They both led me to know Him for who He is.

Each chapter ends with questions to consider to process areas in your life. Ask the Lord how He would have you process your answers, as this is meant for you to be absolutely honest with Him. I am asking the Lord to reveal His extravagant love and compassion for you as you seek Him. You will discover that writing in a journal was a great tool for me. It was helpful because

I was able to look back and tangibly see the Lord's faithfulness to me as I sought Him.

I am asking the Lord to pour out His extravagant love, deliverance, and healing for you as you seek Him in this journey. Find a journal. Be ready to allow Him to minister to you. Record your responses, questions, and prayers. Record His responses of truth and life as He speaks to you. He is the most wonderful Counselor and the greatest One to free us from every prison.

Chapter 1

Voices inside My Head

꧁

A HURTING PERSON who has gone through trauma during his or her childhood, particularly SRA, often has dissociated trauma from their awareness. When dissociation occurs in severity, causing multiple personalities inside one's mind, it's also known as having Dissociative Identity Disorder, formerly known as Multiple Personality Disorder (MPD). The "alters" speak inside the person's mind.

The hurting person lives with parts of her mind dissociated from other parts of her mind. The person experiences constant dialogues inside her mind. Different parts hold trauma, and some parts carry the same related trauma in different ways. Some hold trauma other alters aren't aware of. They talk with other alters inside as well as to the core person. The core person often carries on several conversations inside of her head by different alters at all times. Occasionally, examples of different "voices" may surface as you read, allowing you to have some insight to what they thought during specific situations. Each alter is there for a particular reason and holds a significant aspect of the person's pain.

When one of these voices inside begins to talk with someone, the voice may sound different from the core person. The core person is the main person you are helping. When an alter surfaces, the alter may sound like a younger voice of the core person. The age when the main person experienced the trauma is the age a particular alter represents in their voice. This is also the age of that alter's mental and emotional maturity level.

Different alters may also have different tastes, representing their own personalities. They have different memories and stories making up their identities. Some have different fears. Some are connected with different entities of darkness. All were exposed to incredible hurt and pain. All believed lies about God because of the pain they endured. They believed lies about who He is and who they were resulting from the SRA they experienced.

Following is an example of what an alter said. During this process, examples of what alters said are given as they processed through points of healing. The different font below indicates an alter is "talking."

If they find out I am here, the dragon will be mad. He guards the cage and the ropes tied up around me. No one has seen me. I will be bound and mummified by these ropes from the top of my head to the bottom of my feet forever. No one will ever come to set me free.

This was my reality inside. Maybe it will make more sense to you if I explain what is going on from the perspective of the voice or alter inside. When "we" is used by one who is trapped, it refers to all the alters who live inside of the person's mind. Different alters carry different personalities, memories, and pain. Some of the alters have names. Some don't know what their names are. Some act as leaders or guards representing what is going on inside. Oftentimes, different alters or the core person may speak as "we" when they talk, indicating that they are also speaking of the ones inside of them. This next portion briefly refers to the fear that is strong when the core person is trying to get free from being so trapped.

This alter is inside a cage. Ropes from head to toe tie her up. She is being draped over a pit of horrible things. She cries out to anyone inside to help her. She knows no one who will ever acknowledge she is even there. How can she get out? The Lord will show Himself mighty to save to each alter inside. There were hundreds of alters inside me. Several will tell what they were saying throughout the journey.

Can't let anyone know I am inside.
Will we ever get out? Dragon threatens me again.
Nope.
Cobra is hissing at me.
Someone stop this war of darkness fighting to kill me.
Kelly [alter] is screaming of murder, and Jessica [alter] is trying to rest with the purple fleece blanket. Cassie [alter] is asking for Cheerios®, and Jewels [alter] is trying to prepare for school. Nora [alter] is relaxing with a good book. Amy [alter] is mad, because she didn't get to be with the boy she saw on the way home.

Crowded alters tried to find their place of safety and help inside my head. I didn't remember a time in my life without them. The alters were usually angry and afraid. I tried to help them but didn't know how. I liked them sometimes but mostly didn't. Sometimes I wished they would go away so I didn't have to hear them. I never knew life without headaches, pain, nightmares, physical torment, illness, and trauma from the war of darkness and the voices of alters inside.

During times when I hear alters inside my mind talking, I have learned they are trying to help me. This happens so I don't have to do something I can't handle emotionally. One alter inside of me takes over me just in time. This happens often without my awareness, and I notice the clock is hours later than when I last looked. Sometimes I don't know why or where hours have gone.

I see life going on outside of my cage but can't hear anything except the voices inside. I try to listen but can't hear. Ropes tied around my head keeping me from hearing will have to bust for me to know, hear, and be free.

If the cage opens I might get hurt again. I wouldn't be safe. I see people outside my cage. Meg [alter] said people outside the cage were safe. She said we could get help from people. Not sure. Maybe I am safer here where no one knows what happens. I don't trust people. I wonder why people stand and look like they are praying for us. Why would they pray for us when they don't know us?

I talked. Someone was praying the cage surrounding me would unleash. They talked nice. What will they want from me I cannot give? Will they be like others I know? She sounded like no one I ever heard. What was different? Meg, who tries to help us, said she was safe. I don't trust Meg. The person praying started talking to me. How did she know I was here? She sees me. Maybe she knows I want freedom. Is she safe, or is she another trick?

Maybe someone can help me.

All the ones inside were important. Each served a crucial role in helping me stay alive. The nature of SRA involves various kinds of abuse to an extreme extent. Emotional, mental, physical, sexual, and especially spiritual/demonic activity are all part of Satanic Ritual Abuse. Consequently, an SRA survivor will have tremendous healing to walk through. Total healing and wholeness is possible! Some of these areas are addressed throughout these chapters.

Paralyzed in the Pew

As one heals from DID/SRA, she has particular challenges to work through. This is because the goal of our enemy, Satan, is to destroy the person's mind and heart to ever consider that God is loving or kind. The abuse that takes place in various rituals instills severe distortions about who God is in the person's mind. It causes the person to take on views about herself based on lies from the pit of hell. It is impossible without the hope and mercy of God for her to ever discover that God is on her side.

The enemy of our souls tries everything he can to distort everything about God and His ways. The enemy tries to twist and pervert the significance of who God is. One healing from DID/SRA often has an extremely difficult time in church or being part of anything related to the church of Jesus Christ. God came to heal us in every way.

At one time different alters talk inside the person's mind about walking in the doors of a church. Distortions and tremendous confusion affect how one with SRA may respond to various symbolic emblems in church. Going to church can be scary for her. It is difficult for her to understand a new church isn't like what she may have experienced before. She remembers churches where some rituals of the abuse took place. Symbols intended to draw us closer to Jesus Christ are used in satanic rituals to distort who Jesus Christ is and to abuse the person. Symbols such as Bibles, altars, the color red especially used to represent Christ's blood, crosses, Communion elements, candles, baptismal tanks, and so forth often steer her into a memory or trigger.

She remembers rituals when the enemy taught her who Jesus is to be and what was required of her. The enemy only lied to her. Her beliefs about who Jesus is were all based on the enemy's schemes to use her as a pawn in his darkness to ultimately destroy her. Jesus Christ was and is Victor over all these lies. The enemy was attempting to use her in his kingdom of darkness for keeps. God knew her before the enemy ever came on the scene in her life. God had a plan and purpose for the person before the foundations of the world. She would come to know God for who He really is. Much healing takes place between her bondage and knowing the One who breaks forth for her. In the meantime, the following statements are an example of what different alters have said during encounters at church.

Is the cross on the wall one I have to get on soon?

Why are there so many lights?

The baptismal isn't ready. They have it covered. Who is going to go under in the yucky stuff next?

The flowers on chair seats are nice. Can I sit here?

I thought you said this place was safe!

What is the white linen cloth hanging on both sides of the wooden part? They didn't put the white linen on the cross I had to be on.

Are you sure it is safe in here?

Will they do mean things in here? Why are all the people shaking hands and giving out paper things when you walk in?

I don't want to have to sign anything in blood.

The men are wearing black suits. I don't want to be here.

I hate the lady's red dress.

H-Y-M-N-A-L. What is a hymnal? Is my name written in there, like they put it in their other book?

Flickering candles. How come they aren't arranged like the meetings?

The hangers are all empty. Who's wearing the capes?

Why are there instruments up front? Are they going to burn them?

Why are kids laughing and having fun? Don't they know one day it's their turn? How are they laughing with friends?

If it gets to be too much, Joy said we would leave. Kelly is frightened.

Joy said that if we make it till the end, we will go have ice cream.

I want rocky road!

Rocky road is gross, chocolate chip cookie dough is the best.

I don't like nuts.

No ice cream, I want a doughnut.

We probably won't get anything 'cause others will whine and cause her to decide to leave. Quit your dreaming 'cause you'll be disappointed anyways.

I want electric blue flavor.

Yeah, I want that kind too.

The example above describes what's going on inside someone shattered while in a church setting. It's important to realize the intensity of chaos, confusion, and the demonic influences inside. Each different statement and question represents different alters inside. All of these voices are being voiced consecutively while in church. If a hurting person described this as what she experiences when she goes to church, what would you say? What do you imagine the Lord to say concerning what the person tells you? How might you respond while she expressed her fears and feelings of being trapped? When she thought she couldn't let anyone know because she can't trust anyone, what would be helpful to tell her?

Where is April [alter]? What is happening to Beautiful [alter] and Star [alter]? I don't want to think about the coffin. Why does the coffin keep opening and closing with them putting living things inside? When they make me go in, will I ever come out?

The evil keeps shouting at me when I try to find who might be safe. He starts shouting when it gets better with one inside. He causes more chaos for others to make them upset. There is probably no hope for someone like me.

As alters inside are brought to new understandings of who Jesus Christ of Nazareth is, conflict may arise in them. The enemy against them protests. Not only does the enemy lose them potentially out of his kingdom, but he also knows once they discover who God really is, they become a threat against the enemy. The enemy never wants alters inside to see the truth of who Jesus Christ is. Satan will do anything in his power to keep them from knowing the true Lord Jesus Christ of Nazareth. The enemy knows Jesus Christ is the only One who can help them instead of the darkness they have entrusted themselves to. Often when alters inside have agreed with the darkness and deception of the enemy, they have also attached themselves with demons. They believe demons will help them and be their friends when no one else has helped them thus far.

As alters begin to develop trust with a helper who knows Jesus Christ and they learn that person is safe, they may begin to share the pain they hold. As they begin to share lies they believe, the suffering they experience will also be revealed. The Lord exposes the pain in His perfect timing. When they see who Jesus Christ truly is, they may decide to let Him help them instead of the darkness they have committed to spiritually. They tell the darkness to leave them. They decide to be on the Good Shepherd's side instead of the side of darkness. The following is an example of this taking place with an alter and how other alters responded to the decision.

Stupid April let the friend go poof. She made it go away 'cause she said she wanted to be on the other side, the side that was safe. Little did she know that the darkness was the only thing I believed was a real help. And she just decided to let go of it.

I heard the lady help her and ask her if she was willing to let go of the "darkness," as she called it, for just five seconds and take the hand of Jesus. Stupid April went for it! What was she thinking? Doesn't she know that now we are really in trouble for any help at all because they were one of our friends? Now that they are gone, there must be no help for me.

Yeah, it is quieter here now. I do not hear the venomous threats he would whisper inside of here. But is he really gone forever like they said he was, or is he still hiding around the corner about to punish me because I talked about him? I didn't like him. He was mean and scary.

Any decision an alter makes for truth and for becoming a child of the Kingdom of Light is significant. It is always a big deal when anyone comes to know Jesus Christ personally. God loves nothing more than to have people invite Him into their lives and lead them for the rest of their days. He is ecstatic when someone who has Dissociative Identity Disorder and a background of Satanic Ritual Abuse puts her broken trust into the heart of the living God and asks Him to save her. He answers. He saves her when she asks. He comes, heals, and transforms her when she chooses to follow Him with everything she has.

Consider areas you long to minister concerning those who are shattered. Ask the Lord what role you may have in the lives of those who are broken and hurting. Ask the Lord to begin to prepare your heart for His ministry. Ask the Lord what areas He wants you to discover about Him and His heart for those who are broken. Be willing to hear from Him as you keep turning these pages. He is always speaking to us. Are we always listening?

Questions to Consider

1. What areas in your life have been shattered?

2. What does the Lord still long to heal you of?

3. Ask the Lord how He desires to heal you in each of these areas.

4. Keep a journal of how the Lord begins to meet you in each of the areas you have specifically named.

5. Are you willing to allow the Lord to shed His light, truth, and comfort to places in your life where you've been shattered?

6. Ask the Lord to reveal attitudes you may have that do not reflect the heart of the Lord.

7. How do you want Him to change you or minister to you specifically as you read this book? Tell Him. Record in your journal how He does this as you keep reading and processing with Him.

Chapter 2

Captive to Internal Chaos

My dark horse never quit moving. The horse held secrets for us, so we couldn't share with anyone. His gait was always going faster and faster. When we rode him no one knew our secrets. He just kept going. At times all four of his hooves were off the arena floor, and we felt like we were going to fly. We rode for our dear lives, knowing we would eventually get bucked off and fall to the ground, but we wouldn't cry. We couldn't cry. Crying wasn't allowed, but laughing was, as though nothing at all happened. Moving right along, quickly spot the stirrups again and get back on that spirited horse that ran too fast for us.

MAYBE YOU KNOW someone who is hurting. Maybe you know one who seems to speak riddles to you, leaving you thinking you don't know what she means when she says certain things. With an example of a riddle spoken by an alter, allow me to unpack what this alter was feeling. She was feeling fear, afraid to expose what she held inside. Often those with dissociation are also very creative, as are analogies presented when they describe what's happening inside them.

Molly, another alter, denies the memory as it has surfaced to the other alter. Painting it blurrier, she tries to make it so what has really taken place cannot ever be seen for what it was. She doesn't want to ever tell about the memory. She pretends as though it never happened.

Molly uses the horse to describe her feelings. She makes the "horse" hold the secrets for us. However, when an alter is involved to help hold the secrets, they may not be on the side of the Good Shepherd. When an alter still in darkness tries to help the core person, it causes more confusion and doesn't help the person find freedom. The person may think the alter is helping, as the alters have helped her survive to this point. However, deception of the enemy won't allow the person to see she will never be free as long as alters are still in darkness. This may result in the person being tempted to not make the decision to rid herself of the demonic forces that strongly influence her and her healing.

In the description of Molly and the horse, her feelings of being out of control correspond with the horse going faster and faster. When she fell off the horse she knew she had to get back on. Her feelings of being trapped showed she had nowhere else to go but wherever the horse went. The enemy inside is represented by the horse.

The horse wasn't really being nice to them anymore as they kept getting bucked off. But it was also the horse that helped hold the secrets. They didn't realize they had a choice concerning whether or not they rode the horse. They thought the horse was the one who protected them from letting the secrets out. They believed if the secrets got out they would die. They're taught they must stay on the horse even if it runs too fast for them and they are riding out of control. They believe they have no other choice.

As you can see in this situation, the feelings of being trapped and bound to specific secrets, vows, or entities creates much chaos and conflict inside of the person. Each alter tries to perform her particular "jobs" (holding denial, protecting, holding specific memories, etc.). Alters may also have various secrets and vows with those who have hurt them, as well as the demons who have acted as "friends" to them in order to keep them in bondage.

I discovered tidbits of truth during the most difficult times. It was not believable to me yet. I didn't like Scripture. However, it seemed to get to my pain like nothing else could. I didn't know why, yet.

But this is a people plundered and despoiled; all of them are trapped in caves, or are hidden away in prisons; they have become a prey with none to deliver them, and a spoil, with none to say, "Give them back!"

—Isaiah 42:22

For He looked down from His holy height; from heaven the LORD gazed upon the earth, to hear the groaning of the prisoner; to set free those who were doomed to death.

—Psalm 102:19–20

Let the groaning of the prisoner come before You; according to the greatness of Your power preserve those who are doomed to die.

—Psalm 79:11

How blessed is the man whose strength is in You; in whose heart are the highways to Zion! Passing through the valley of Baca they make it a spring; The early rain also covers it with blessings. They go from strength to strength, every one of them appears before God in Zion.

—Psalm 84:5–7

During times of chaos I wrote. Journal entries will be included in italics from over the years of finding healing.

When pain is like this I don't know what to think about Jesus. I don't know what's true about Him when it hurts. Darkness told me Jesus doesn't care. They said Jesus was a joke. They reminded me of all the times "Jesus" was in ceremonies of darkness and never came to rescue me. The Jesus in ceremonies only hurt me. What if He doesn't really care? How do I know He is even real?

Does He care when I hurt? Will He cause aches I feel inside to go away? It is easy to think that I must deserve the pain and the punishment that may come my way. But I don't know what is true about this. I want out. I wonder if I can be free from being roped up from head to toe. Will anyone ever be able to unleash me from the ropes inside my captive soul? My tear-stained pillow is my companion. It hurts when layers and covers are removed in the night.

Who can heal this? Will I be captive forever? I don't want to continue to live only to discover I will never be whole or healed. Is there a healing balm to come soothe and heal my soul forever?

Even as I write this I am reminded of a time when I was so desperate for the "autumn rains" to come and make my soul to be a place of springs. That seemed too good to be true as I remember night after night dreaming of a life where there would be no secrets, no shame, no fear, no despair, and no torment. I didn't know how long my hope would last. I tried to tenaciously believe that one day, life would be different. I didn't know when I would have moments of freedom. I didn't know if freedom would ever take place. I didn't know if I would ever be glad to be alive. The one person I did know was the God of the Ages. The all-powerful God of the Bible continually promised He heard me every one of these nights.

During nights of crying out to Him, reminding Him of the promises He consistently brought to me, I felt like I was making a mockery of God. I felt no matter how hard I tried to get free, it didn't work. I wasn't getting free. I was embarrassed to think I was just trusting that one day I would be free because God promised. I was so afraid that if God promised freedom and freedom never came, I would make a liar out of Him. I desperately wanted healing and freedom quickly, instantaneously, and on my terms.

By His grace, I came to freedom through a great process, a pilgrimage. As I have passed through the valley of Baca (the place of grieving, mourning, processing, and engaging with many memories), the place of spring has come into my soul. The autumn rains also cover it with pools. I have gone from strength to strength as I have discovered who He is and who I am as a result. I know He hears my prayers and looks on me with favor.

As this process was taking place, I didn't know if I would ever know a different life, much less the life of freedom that I craved. I thought I was absolutely losing my mind. I thought I would end up in a hospital, crazy. Keeping busy with seemingly mindless activities such as sports and school-related events occupied me most of the time, so I didn't have to recognize the raging war in my mind. I felt like I had an excuse not to listen to what was going on in my mind because of the other distractions and activities I filled it with. Activities of practicing basketball in the gym, running a better time on the track, swimming another lap, or working the evening shift kept me occupied so the battle in my mind wasn't as intense. When I wasn't doing anything the voices seemed louder and more tormenting. Still, I could always hear them even in my attempts at staying busy.

I am not ready to go home.
I want to stay out with the friend and practice some more shooting.
I just want to go to bed.

Where is the teddy? Is he still safe on the bed where I left him?

I want some Cheerios.

Can I have some candy?

Can I wear a different shirt now 'cause you let another one have her turn with that color today. Is it my turn now?

Why can't you shut up and keep quiet about everything? You're letting the cat out of the bag. You're not supposed to say anything.

I am going to get the razor.

I can't get anyone to love me.

Can someone help me?

Does anyone hear me?

Rock, rock back and forth, back and forth. The purples and blues and blacks swirl inside. No one will miss me. Six feet isn't so far down.

We are going to get married to the high priest tonight. Is the cape ready?

I don't want to go.

Can't anyone rescue me from having to go?

I spot the yellow patch of the Starburst wrapper. Even though it's safe here, it isn't always safe. It will be there in case one night, darkness comes again. I can look at it until they all stop. The new quilt I bought is my comfort.

Other times my own thoughts would be louder than the others, but the majority of the time they felt like they were drowning among the other voices, and I would usually have to write down my own.

My mind races through the day's events that have previously passed. Seems like such a long day at work. I don't like bosses who yell at me or co-workers who tell me how to do things when I have been there longer. Why can't they just leave me alone? Why can't they do their jobs and let me do mine? Why does everyone have to look over my shoulder into my business when it is not theirs to look into? Why couldn't you let us go on the drive so I knew it was safe a couple more hours before darkness inside began to bother me?

Hopefully, tonight will be better: better rest, better dreams. Maybe the darkness won't want to ask me tonight. Maybe the covers on my bed won't smother me, and I can take them all off when I want to. Even though they're heavy on top of me, they won't make me work hard for something. Maybe my brown eyes can stay closed without a bondage breaking my brief silence.

Maybe I will get past the three o'clock hour without any scary interruptions. If I don't, maybe it will be easier this time to rest on the pillow until the sun rises. Why is it that the sun gets to sleep, yet I can't? Why does darkness always seem to visit when I don't want them to? They always keep me up. Don't they have anyone else to bother at that hour?

I will be sure to wash my face more, so in the morning no one will notice if it has signs of being tired. What would people think if they knew my encounters of the night were keeping me from sleeping? They would think I was going crazy. I can't let them know. When will freedom seep into the holes of this cage? Will the ropes ever come off?

> With whom My hand will be established; My arm also will strengthen him. The enemy will not deceive him, nor the son of wickedness afflict him. But I shall crush his adversaries before him, and strike those who hate him. And My faithfulness and My lovingkindness will be with him, and in My name his horn will be exalted.
>
> —Psalm 89:21–24

There is no way that any of this is going to really happen, this freedom that I keep reading about in the Bible. Even though one thing seems to go well in my circumstances, it ends up that it doesn't work out after all. What is the purpose of believing that something will really happen and then it doesn't happen when I want it to? My circumstances scream that I can't be free.

I am so tired of being stranded and being hopeless in the meantime. This is never going to end. I feel like I will never know a mind without loud, threatening, chaotic voices inside of me.

Jesus, it seems like You have turned to visit the silence of those nights where even the stars have hidden until twinkle time again. Jesus, I know You're here. I know You're closer than my skin. Sometimes it is difficult to believe when my nights continue to fill with more questions than answers. I confess to You I am weary of asking again. Show me if You're real.

> If the LORD had not been my help, my soul would soon have dwelt in the abode of silence.
>
> If I should say, "My foot has slipped," Your loving-kindness, O LORD, will hold me up. When my anxious thoughts multiply within me, Your consolations delight my soul.
>
> —Psalm 94:17–19

> I, even I, am He who comforts you. Who are you that you are afraid of man who dies and of the son of man who is made like grass, that you have forgotten the LORD your Maker, who stretched out the heavens and laid the foundations of the earth, that you fear continually all day long because of the fury of the oppressor as he makes ready to destroy? But where is the fury of the oppressor? The exile will soon be set free, and will not die in the dungeon, nor will his bread be lacking.
>
> —Isaiah 51:12–14

> Thus says the LORD, "In a favorable time I have answered you, and in a day of salvation I have helped you; and I will keep you and give you for a covenant of the people, to restore the land, to make them inherit the desolate heritages; saying

to those who are bound, "Go forth," to those who are in darkness, "Show yourselves." Along the roads they will feed, and their pasture will be on all bare heights."

—Isaiah 49:8–9

One with DID/SRA may continue to wrestle with the emotional chaos in her life until she is whole and free. During these times of upheaval her daily life is also chaotic. This causes her daily routines to be inconsistent and filled with crises. This is normal for one who is struggling to be healed and free. I always thought I was the only one who thought my life and my mind were crazy. I believed no one else would understand how incredibly unstable my daily life was. I feared my life would always be in crisis and never be "normal." Let me assure you, if you are struggling to get freedom, there is hope, total healing, and freedom for you! God is no respecter of persons. He doesn't play favorites. His heart is to heal and set all of us free. God really did heal and set me free! It was not always an easy process, nor did it happen overnight, but it did happen.

The next chapter will shed further light on the inconsistencies of daily life because one with DID/SRA often loses time. Depending on where the person is in healing, this can range from losing weeks and months at a time to moments of time. Losing time is another common trait of one with DID/SRA.

Questions to Consider

1. Jeremiah 31:25 says that the Lord refreshes the weary and satisfies the faint. Write about your weariness. Ask Him to refresh you and satisfy your faint soul.

2. Write down His responses as you hear Him speak to you the next few days.

3. Psalm 34:18 talks about God saving those broken and crushed in spirit. Write about times you were crushed in

spirit. How did God save you during those times? What beauty did you find in Him as He came close to your brokenness?

4. What does the Lord promise us in Isaiah 49:8–11? Write about promises that minister to you.

5. What does this passage reveal to you about God? Does it challenge your previous beliefs about who God is? How?

6. What is your response to the truth that God is intimately aware of what we experience?

7. Lord, is there further healing You desire to complete in my life related to memories or experiences I've had?

Chapter 3

Tripping over Time

ABCs of Being in School

THE MUSIC TEACHER told me, "Here, practice this one more time just to be sure you are ready for the talent show. We only have a couple of practices left before Friday." He handed me the sheet music with the song he wanted me to sing. I read the title of the song and the words that followed. I had never seen this song before. I thought he must have mistaken me for someone else. How could he think I would be ready to sing this in front of everyone in two days? In my mind I rehearsed his words, *Just to be sure you are ready*. Ready for what? I can't sing this song! I have never seen this song in my life before, much less be ready to sing it! What was I going to do? My teacher seemed so confident I was going to be ready to perform. I didn't want to disappoint him. He seemed to think I was doing great. How could I be doing great if I had never seen this song before?

I tried racking my brain as to how he could have thought I was doing so well in previously practicing the piece. I was left confused, like I needed to play catch-up and quickly learn the song without his finding out that I really didn't know it. How could I explain to him I really had no idea how the song was supposed to be sung? How could I tell him he must have had the wrong person in mind when he gave the piece to me?

I hated playing catch-up. It was like I was always cleaning up after someone's "mess," and I didn't know how it got made. I constantly felt like I was covering for someone else, even though I never knew who that someone else was. I hated feeling like I had to make excuses for situations I couldn't figure out how I got into. However, other people who were involved and talking to me seemed to be perfectly aware I belonged in those scenarios.

I didn't know where I was supposed to be when much of the time I found myself covering for different alters' messes and feeling like I had to clean up after them. In order for my own life to make more sense I learned to make lots of great excuses to cover. I lied a lot. I felt I had to say anything to keep others from questioning my life. I knew I would never be able to explain anything. I had little understanding then of what was really taking place in my daily life. The following is a brief description of what particular alters inside said about working on a school assignment.

We have to make an A on this term paper or we will be failures.

I want to go to bed.

Can I sleep with teddy bear tonight 'cause Kelly [alter] threw it on the floor last night. She doesn't like teddy bear.

I don't know why the novel for the paper is so important. It is so boring to listen to as she reads aloud.

The story I like; I want her to keep reading it.

There are not enough references. I need to help her find more resources for the footnotes or we might get docked points. We can't have that. It needs to be done well.

Why can't you just forget the paper and this stupid class? You are going to fail it anyway.

Yeah, this meaningless class is not really important. You are not going to graduate anyway, so you are just wasting your time trying to finish this stupid paper.

Why don't you get rid of the articles? I will help you find something better to do. You don't need to waste your time on this. You are not going to be alive tomorrow anyway, so what is the point of trying to work on something that won't matter when you are dead?

You'll see, you will wish you hadn't wasted your time on this.

I want to read the chapter again 'cause I liked the part about the boy going to the art shop and buying art supplies. Can I have some art supplies? Finger paint and stuff? Please?

Busy at the computer, I was typing, finishing the paper due at the end of the school term. A conversation such as this was taking place at the same time, like a crowd fighting for airtime in my mind. I only had the conclusion of the paper to finish and a couple of last looks for final revisions before handing in the paper before its due date. Two A.M. tick-tocked its way to me. I felt the curtain of my eyelids close over my tired eyes. I was almost done; I just wanted to look at it once more. Copies of journal articles, reference materials, news clippings, and other research material covered my bedroom floor, surrounding my desk filled with term paper residue. I had planned to get up the next morning with a refreshed look at it again before printing.

Greeting me the next morning were papers shredded everywhere, as though someone had been ripping them apart for hours. All I could see were clippings, articles, reviews, and references ripped to pieces. I could not believe what I saw! I didn't want to believe it. I was so close to being completely finished with the paper, and now this? How in the world was I supposed to finish it now with everything shredded? The paper was not on my computer. It had somehow been erased. I didn't know what happened.

I asked my roommate if she knew about what had happened. She said, "Yeah, I wondered what you were doing in the middle of the night. I saw you ripping everything apart. I asked you what was going on and you just started swearing at me, so I didn't want to bother you anymore." I thought, *You didn't want to bother me when my entire semester project was being shredded to pieces? Why didn't you do something?*

Again, I did not know what was happening as different alters would do things, and I felt like I was constantly trying to make up for what was happening. I felt so out of control. I didn't know what the next disaster would be that I would have to somehow figure out how to explain. I didn't know what would be the next thing for me to try to fix or cover up in such a way so no one would suspect such chaos in my life. After all, I wouldn't have known what to tell them.

I always ended up in situations, thinking, *How did I get in the middle of this?* I knew I was losing time and later learned why this was. I wanted to be in control. The conversations in my head led to more confusion in my own understanding. They were not helping.

Meanwhile, I attended school the next day dreading the teacher commenting that the papers were due. To my amazement an emergency occurred in his family, and he had to leave for a couple of weeks. He gave an extension on the due date by telling us to simply turn it in to another teacher in the department. I couldn't believe my ears. That meant I would have a little bit of time at least to try to recover what I had already worked so hard on. Maybe I could turn it in after all. The quality wouldn't be as good, but at least it would be turned in and receive some sort of grade rather than an incomplete. I was so grateful I didn't have to explain anything. Life could go on as "normal."

I looked back at the clock to check the time, and four hours has passed. Four hours? I knew it was just noon a second ago. I was so confused and nearly convinced that the clock on the wall had broken, so I checked another clock in another room. Same time. Hmm. Where had the four hours gone? The last thing I know happened was at noon when I was talking to someone in the office at the pregnancy center. I couldn't figure out what had happened during the lost time. I still thought that the clock must have broken. Maybe both clocks were in the same outlet, so both of the clocks I saw were broken on the same wrong time. What was happening?

I was rummaging through my wallet in search of all the receipts I had gathered from various shopping and different errands over the month. For some reason, not all of my receipts looked familiar. I didn't remember going to the perfume shop, or the art supply store, or getting any clothing as the different receipts indicated. I couldn't figure out why these receipts were in my wallet.

Other times I noticed that my account had been overdrawn and I would be so frustrated when I knew I had been diligent as to what I was purchasing that month and what bills were being paid. Somehow, more money was being spent than I thought, but I couldn't understand how. When my discipline and organization didn't meet the standard of my bank balance I knew something was wrong. This was before I realized I was missing so much time, and different alters were present without my being aware. They would buy their own things and spend money without my knowledge.

Later, I began to realize there were alters who presented themselves during my day. I tried bargaining with them to keep the money situation under control. I told them, even the younger alters, I wouldn't get mad at them for getting something as long as they kept the receipt. At first some of the younger alters didn't even know what a receipt was, so I told them what it was one time when I bought something.

It was still a process. Obviously I didn't grow up concerned about how to manage my money and didn't develop those skills over the years. So as I missed time, whenever an alter decided to get what they wanted, I was still responsible for them and how I would take care of their decisions. This became easier as I talked specifically to different alters inside about how to help the younger ones if they knew more about what was spent than I.

Also, I discovered that if I allowed the alters a specific amount to spend it wasn't as frustrating. They were satisfied with that because they had some of their own money that wouldn't be taken away from them by another alter. They got better at keeping receipts after that because it wasn't as threatening for them to buy something without getting in trouble. This became easier for me also.

Sometimes I was at a familiar place and ran into someone I didn't know, but the other person insisted she knew me. She might say, "Don't you remember? I met you at the café," or the gym, or the bar, or some other place I didn't remember. I never quite knew what to do, other than say, "Oh yeah!" and quickly change the subject after smiling and nodding. This was especially awkward if I was with a friend and she may be wondering, "What were you doing there with her?" Whenever I was confronted, I typically blew it off and changed the subject or made some excuse as to why I couldn't remember the person who knew me.

The worst was when the other person who acted as though she knew me, called me by a different name, and the friend I was with would laugh because she heard me being called a name she didn't think was mine by someone who acted like she knew me well. I didn't know what else to do other than play along. Then when I was done talking to the "friend," I would explain to my other friend that they really had the wrong person, but I didn't know how to say, "You must have mistaken me for someone else," because she was talking as though she had known me a good while.

I was so confused when this would happen. I never knew how to explain myself to anyone else if they saw encounters like this. It always felt so strange, knowing something was going on inside of me and yet not knowing what was happening. Then, as I began to hear more alters, it was difficult not to betray them. I wouldn't let the "right" alter in me present herself to that person again in fear of having another embarrassing situation, especially if someone was with me.

Until later in my healing, when I missed time I usually wouldn't know it until after the fact. When I had noticed I had missed time I always felt completely disoriented. Sometimes I would be absent for hours at a time. Other times it would be a couple of days. Other times it would be for several moments.

If I was aware an alter was presenting herself or "out" (the person people see when they are interacting with me) and I knew I was missing time because of this, I didn't really want the alter to be out because she would do and say things I didn't want. During these times, I tried so hard to come to the surface and be at the forefront again, but often this didn't happen. I knew I wanted to talk and be the one to represent myself in whatever situation was happening. I felt so trapped and frozen inside whenever I could not be at the front. The best way I know how to describe this feeling is being underwater, hearing all the voices above the water and seeing all that is happening above the water. However, I could never rise and engage with the reality of what was happening above the water. I always felt trapped by the weights of the darkness.

I felt stupid asking myself questions concerning my surroundings when I knew I should know the answers already, such as "How did I get here? What am I doing here? What am I supposed to be doing here? Where do I know these people from? How can I best blend into this place and situation even though I don't know how I got here or what I am doing here?" Yet it seemed every time this happened everyone else always seemed to know what I was doing there and what was going on. I felt even more awkward about telling them I didn't know what was happening.

Everyone seemed to know for some reason I was supposed to be there even though I often had no clue what to do once I discovered myself out of context. Then I was "back," presenting myself, yet I did not know what had taken place in the in-between times. Sometimes when I didn't know what I was doing somewhere I "played stupid" in a sarcastic way to let other people think that I was joking about my questions. Yet in doing so, they often joked back with a semi-serious answer to play along. It was enough of a clue for me to understand a bit of what was happening in my surroundings. I tried to ask questions without letting them know I was temporarily trying to gather my surroundings and make sense of what I was doing somewhere after a period of missed time.

During stages of my healing, I would be extremely confused as to whether or not I could really be free from my bondage. I often couldn't be the one to express I wanted to be free. Instead, an alter inside would often say things such as the following:

I am not going to ever be free anyway, so I don't want to talk anymore. So don't ever call me again. I don't want to tell anybody anything anymore. Forget it.

When I heard they were making comments like this I would become so frustrated and discouraged. I felt like I couldn't really express my own feelings when they were exploding like cannons inside of me. I often felt jealous of alters inside when they seemed to be able to articulate more clearly than I about despair consuming me.

When I was around other people, the alters and all their emotions drowned my own. Questions kept my mind company among the chorus of voices. The alters didn't trust. They hated it when I said stuff I thought. They didn't want a person I was talking to knowing they were inside of me. I couldn't really tell her what was happening. If I let on to her that conversations constantly took place in my mind she would just think I was crazy. She may have thought I needed to be locked up in a mental institution somewhere. I always thought no one would understand what happened inside of me. Some people just thought I was quiet as others comfortably socialized and interacted with other people. Usually I just sat back and didn't say much, not because I didn't want to. I was usually trying to calm the alters' conversations that were already taking place in my mind.

Sometimes I felt like I couldn't get a word in edgewise in my own head because of all the confusion, arguments, and disagreements at any given time. Sometimes I felt like a mother in the sense that I felt as though I often ended up calming alters inside as I mediated the arguing and confusion taking place. This was all in hopes it would prevent an alter from being upset and coming to the front, letting someone know what was happening inside. That could be a very embarrassing situation, and it happened many times!

Then I was caught thinking, *How in the world can I graciously explain the "voice" that was not my own voice, but one inside my head that communicated something entirely out of place for the social situation I was physically in?* As first I discovered that doing this in such a way to not offend or embarrass the alters could be a challenge. I really just wanted to completely dismiss that anything had taken place. However, the other person and I both knew that what took place was not necessarily normal in interactions for most people in social gatherings. I was preoccupied with trying to mediate and talk silently to the alters according to the conversations taking place at any given time. I didn't mind that people thought I was quiet. It was easier to let them think that than to explain, "I am listening to the voices inside my head!"

Losing time was a normal occurrence for me. Sometimes I still catch myself looking at the clock wondering if I missed time or if I just don't remember everything I did in the last hour. Now I know it is just because I didn't remember every detail of the hour, and it is normal. I don't lose time anymore. I never realized how much of life I missed out on because of losing time. I knew I was becoming more healed when I recognized living hours of the day and night I never had before. I noticed my life was becoming better when I was aware of where I was and didn't feel as though I was in a mental fog all the time.

I cherished times in my healing process when I would recognize for the first time I had transitioned from one appointment to another, kept a day planner, and remembered every item on the schedule for that day. This had never happened in the early stages of healing. But as the Lord began to heal me, He allowed me to not be afraid anymore to live out what He had for me during every part of the day. No alter inside needed to live it for me anymore as He continued to heal me. This took time.

I will never forget the first time I looked at the clock to be sure I would be ready to go somewhere in about an hour. I was afraid I had lost time because the clock was two hours past the time I was expecting. I was so discouraged to think that after all the healing, how could an alter have lived the last two hours and me not be aware? During the later stages of my healing I was aware when the alters were "out" and I was no longer unconscious of this. I was frustrated and wondered if I was as far in my healing as I had thought. I went into another room to get ready because I was now late to the appointment. I was still trying to figure out how I had lost the two hours when I noticed another clock and it was two hours prior to the other clock. Really? I was momentarily elated. Maybe I hadn't missed time. I was so excited and curious I called my friend to ask her the time to be super sure I had the right time on my second clock. She knew my struggles with losing time, so she knew why I asked. She told me the time. It really had been two hours earlier than I thought. My first clock was broken. I had never been so excited my clock was really broken, and I was becoming more healed!

Questions to Consider

1. What are times in your life when you felt as though you missed out emotionally or felt you weren't able to engage as you wished to?

2. Write and tell the Lord about these areas. He knows these times intimately. Tell the Lord what you desired for these times.

3. Ask the Lord how healing can take place in these times.

4. Search in Scripture for situations that seemed as though the timing fit for what the Lord did or didn't do. Ask the Lord in each passage to show you His heart for these times.

5. Ask the Lord to restore those areas and give you hope for what was lost during those times and joy for what He still has for you.

6. Ask the Lord how grief may be part of this healing process.

7. What appointed time has the Lord called you to now?

Chapter 4

Talking about Triggers

OFTEN TIMES WHEN an alter is triggered and begins to surface or be "out," the person is unaware. As a result, this can be extremely embarrassing to the core person because she is trying to regain control but may feel helpless because she can't get to the surface as the core person herself.

The raging inside remembers glass cups shattered on bathroom floors. I cut my hair and put it in newspaper sacks I received every single morning. I made the vow I would never marry again.

Time is alive. It wasn't back then. Time is as though it's happening again. Right now. Senses inside know when the time doesn't replay but lives our existence over and over and over again. The pain isn't dead. It is living to suffocate.

Black curtains greeted me on one side as I proceeded to walk into the church where I had to go to a meeting. Farther inside were long tables covered with candles and black tablecloths, and a variety of junk food goodies. Up front was a plethora of several candles on both sides of the stage. I knew I couldn't stay. I walked in, in spite of alters yelling at me for even thinking about going in after the greeting by black curtains. I tried to persuade the alters it wouldn't be bad by grabbing a plastic plate and filling it with animal crackers and cookies. My method of calming them down worked as long as it took to eat the goodies!

Then my friend came by and asked how I was doing. I told her, "Fine. Want an animal cracker?" I didn't know how to explain that I was afraid of the candles inside the room. Fortunately, she knew about my background so a few moments into our conversation I said I was feeling uncomfortable and needed to get some fresh air. "I wish there weren't so many lit candles in there." She asked if I had told anyone, hoping they could be blown out. I told her, "No, because if I did say anything it would sound strange to them, and they probably wouldn't do anything anyway." When the intern talked to me, he wasn't concerned about what could be done, even though he could have had the candles extinguished. He was only interested in whether or not I was over my problem. He simply shrugged his shoulders and said, "I'm sure you'll be fine. We think the candles need to stay the way they are." I felt stupid, unprotected, mocked, and trapped to stay or else I would be penalized, as attendance was required for internship. I could not get past all my anguish and alters being extremely triggered.

The curtains look like the ones they laid across the table for the sacrifice.
Be porcelain-doll face and don't let anyone get to us.
We should have put on the overalls and make it hard to get to us if we go on the altar.
Church won't ever be safe.
Who is the one needing to be sacrificed?
Is this where the babies die?

I hate the singing.

They must be part of the darkness if they made fun of me.

There will never be anything to sing about in a church.

I couldn't stay in church. I walked out and found a place at another table to calm the chaos inside. I knew if I stayed I wouldn't be able to remain without being triggered and alters coming to the surface. I didn't want to have any embarrassing moments there. They would kick me out of their program. My goal was to keep myself together and not let the alters "out." If I couldn't, I knew I needed to leave.

I missed time during church meetings. Once I noticed this, I didn't want to continue losing time. I knew I had to leave. I was not making it. Alters were too upset inside. I knew the reality was nothing bad would happen to me there. I wasn't far enough in my healing process to calm the alters down effectively when they were triggered.

When situations looked like they were related to darkness and reminded me of satanic rituals similar to past circumstances, the alters were triggered back to a memory. I finally left midway through the second worship song. I asked them what was making them upset.

They had no problems telling me.

The communion tray must be full of blood.

We don't want to have to drink the blood.

Whenever they passed the cup around it was always blood.

I don't want to participate.

They are getting quiet, passing the tray, and I don't want to have to drink it again!

Just flip the tray and make it spill everywhere.

If I make the tray crash all over the floor, we won't have to have any of it.

Just wait till it gets to us and their communion time will be over.

We want to blow the candles out, but they won't let us.

They won't blow them out after we asked nicely.

It is dark like the times when the spirits come and take over and make us do bad things.

Can we have pizza after?

Just give Molly [alter] bubblegum and make her be quiet.

Though this was a difficult situation for me, I believe it had gone through the filter of the Lord and was allowed for a purpose. He continued to show me my need for extensive healing. I didn't appreciate His purposes at the time and would have rather not been in those situations. Often when I was triggered, I found those times very telling of my view of God concerning what happened.

I believe it is always God's desire to reveal His true character to us. I no longer believe I am excluded from seeing His true character and heart. When I was triggered, part of the reason it happened at those particular times was because it was His time to reveal incorrect perceptions I had about God. The truth sets us free. God desires for us to be free from distortions preventing us from walking in His truth. These distortions needed to be brought to the surface before I could absorb His truth.

Unless I was willing to acknowledge what I believed, incorrect or truthful, I was not in a position to allow the Lord to change these beliefs. I learned I did not have to keep beliefs I didn't want. I began praying, "Lord, I don't want to keep beliefs I have about____." As I took a closer look at lies I believed, I was more able to acknowledge what was truth and what were lies. As the Holy Spirit faithfully showed me His truth, He challenged lies I believed.

God had me go through this situation so more of His truth and true character could be revealed. The truth is that He is absolutely delighted in where I was with Him. He saw I was continually growing and desiring His truth. He saw I wanted to please Him, and He was giving me grace. If someone else had walked in my shoes for long, they probably would have had a difficult time with the same scenario I was faced with. No one I knew then had experienced what I had.

The truth is that just because I have a difficult time when I am triggered, it doesn't mean I am not continuing to progress. The Lord desires to move me forward in healing. If the lies I believe about Him and myself are exposed, I am able to receive His truth to take away the lies I believed. When I am triggered, it is an avenue the Lord uses to continue to move me forward. I am asked to face what I believe about Him and myself.

Also, when a spiritual struggle occurs and feelings of discouragement set in, a person can go one of two ways. The first way is listening to thoughts and believing them without thinking about whether or not they are true. This road can lead to believing lies from the enemy. The enemy will often place strategic thoughts in our heads, especially during times of struggle, getting us to believe we are defeated and have no hope. This is why it is crucial to understand the enemy's schemes, lest we be taken captive by them, unaware of how the enemy attacks.

How do we understand the enemy's schemes? Draw near to the Lord, and He will give us the increased understanding, knowledge, and insight to open our spiritual eyes. As we draw near to the Lord, we are equipped to resist the enemy and cause him to flee from us because we are equipped with truth, the Word of God. The Sword of the Spirit is the ammunition that defeats the enemy's tactics in our lives.

The other road we can take after a trigger situation filled with lies is to pause and consider what we are thinking. When we take thoughts captive and sift what is true and what are lies, we can choose to believe what is true. This can be difficult at first to exercise. For so long you may have been used to always believing your own thoughts. Now it is time to distinguish between truths and lies.

Recovering from Being Tripped by the Trigger

The lady was wearing red pants and I knew in my mind she wouldn't hurt me. Alters kept yelling and screaming to get away. The whole time I kept wondering why I was still struggling with seeing her in red pants, because I thought this trigger was not painful to me anymore.

When I watched the movie with friends, all the lights went out so we could see the movie better. I compulsively wanted to escape. I didn't know why. I felt so silly feeling this instead of having a "normal" response of flicking off the lights to see the movie.

When a person experiences triggers as described above, it is helpful to be aware that they don't happen in vain. It is an opportunity for her to know truth instead of the lies she believes in the circumstances causing her to be triggered. Often triggers indicate a flashback of a particular memory that causes the person to switch to an alter who has undergone the memory being triggered. When this happens, some questions a helper might ask are, "Who inside is struggling? Are you remembering something in particular? Does this situation remind you of something that happened? Does someone inside know how to help [the person's name] be strong again [so they can be present]?"

Depending on the situation, it is sometimes helpful to talk to the core person if she can get strong enough to present herself again. Other times it may be appropriate to work with the alter who was triggered. Often, alters have difficulty trusting people and feeling safe. Use caution in talking to them if they feel threatened. It helps them if you are not alarmed. Try to protect the person by using grace and keeping the environment as non-embarrassing for them as possible.

When an alter in this situation is triggered and begins to voice what she's thinking, it can be an awkward scenario if those around don't know what is happening. It's important as helpers to not get offended at what an alter may be saying. The beliefs and memories alters hold are significant to the person's healing process. Let's say, for example, the alter starts yelling and she's angry. Perhaps she throws things and curses at you. Maybe it is your first experience in seeing an alter surface. Maybe you are just as frightened as she is because you "don't know her anymore" and she "doesn't know you."

What are some things you could do in this situation? Pray. Ask the Lord what this precious alter needs to know and hear. Questions a helper could ask may be, "How can I help you right now? I see you are upset about something," or, "I would like to help you. Can you tell me what is bothering you right now?" If the alter doesn't know what is upsetting her, maybe another alter inside is aware of what happened that caused this other alter to come to be out. Questions like, "Does someone else inside know what is bothering you right now? Would they like to talk about what is happening right now?"

If the alter begins to share what is upsetting her, it is important to reassure the alter and the person they're safe. Tell them you are listening. Tell them they will not be in trouble if they say what is bothering them. Depending on how much the alter says, ask if she knows the Good Shepherd or if she knows who the Good Shepherd is.

So often after an alter shares, or when the person herself tells you what's wrong, the accuser of the brethren will immediately begin to lie to her. He may tell her what she shared is ludicrous, you really don't care, and she'll be in trouble now. When you as a helper are aware of some of the schemes the enemy uses against hurting people, you can effectively combat the enemy's intentions by declaring truth as you talk with them. Truths directly going against lies hurled by the enemy to the hurting person may compromise the potency of the lies when they pierce the person's spirit.

I was volunteering at a local pregnancy center as part of my university requirements, thinking I would be there for a year. While going through part of my training to be a pregnancy counselor, I watched several videos about fetal development and learned about the birth process. It involved graphic details and video footage.

At first I thought it was fascinating as I learned how babies developed in such detail until they reached full-term growth. A couple of weeks into my training, every time I watched the videos and read accompanying materials I began to have excruciating pain. I thought initially the lunch I had eaten recently must be the problem. I didn't want to think my pain was related to anything more. However, in spite of my wishes, cramping continued. It was followed by a series of various flashbacks and nightmares of screaming bloody babies and echoes of abortions. Triggers and memories flooded my mind of what I was forced to do to babies of my own. I didn't know what to process. I knew I was constantly having horrible dreams I didn't know what to make of. The situation got to a point where I wondered if my body was remembering something I couldn't recall. I knew my mind was disturbed.

I named her Holly 'cause she was born near Christmas.

I wanted to tie ribbons in her hair when she got older, but they made me tie ropes around her.

I wonder if her favorite color would have been purple like mine.

I wanted to be a nice mommy and take care of her.

She is with the others who had to go on the altar. They are all safe now and will never be hurt again.

I saw her playing tag with the lambs He takes care of. They go baa-baa and she is laughing. I never saw her laugh before.

I didn't want to do any of it. If I told any of what happened, would anyone believe me?

I can't tell anyone ever what happened. They will not believe me.

They will just think we are crazy.

I wanted to love the baby and hold it and feed it. They wouldn't let me.

They took her. Will they take everything precious to me?

Good Shepherd gave her pretty ribbons for her hair. He knows just how she likes it beautifully braided.

Will she ever know I loved her but was never allowed to show her or tell her?

Didn't Jesus think I would have been a good mommy?

I would have saved up to get her a rocking horse or a dollhouse if she wanted.

Why did they make me hurt her?

What would her smile have been like?

I wonder if she would have liked taking ballet.

She is dancing with the angels now, she is swirling in the dress Good Shepherd made for her, light pink that flows with her as she twirls.

One day I finally wrote what I thought would be a confidential note to a lady who I was volunteering with regarding talking to her about some thoughts that I was having. She was willing to talk with me. Shortly into our conversation she asked if I had had an abortion. I honestly wasn't sure at that point, considering the nightmares I was having. I didn't remember giving birth, but this was what the alters were all screaming about. My mind kept remembering the training videos. I knew something was really wrong inside. Volunteering there didn't work out because it became a trigger for me and too much for me to handle. I didn't necessarily realize it then, but this was a key trigger the Lord used to eventually propel my understanding to what was really going on inside, as well as the trauma concerning what happened related to SRA.

I am running. My arms trail by my side down the carpeted aisle where the newborn babies were getting dedicated. Hate them all. They have beautiful small faces of blue eyes and no blood on them. Why couldn't mine still be alive and with no blood on them?

Get them to stop crying. Will their mommies stop their babies' crying?

I didn't make them cry. Panic.

One is laughing. I try to go faster out of the double doors of the church as they sing as though they were rejoicing and it's all bliss to them. They sing songs about the cross, about it being wonderful.

My feet go as fast as they can, making heads turn towards me. I see their suits and ties. Outside in the foyer I don't recognize the paintings on the wall. Mind swirls of confusion. Colors of grays and purples and blacks invade the holes of time that I am missing.

> But you, Israel, My servant, Jacob whom I have chosen, descendant of Abraham My friend, you whom I have taken from the ends of the earth, and called from its remotest parts and said to you, "You are My servant, I have chosen you and not rejected you. Do not fear, for I am with you; do not anxiously look about you, for I am your God. I will strengthen you, surely I will help you, surely I will uphold you with My righteous right hand.
>
> —Isaiah 41:8–10

I never would have imagined the Lord healing me in each of those triggers and memories that the triggers stirred inside my soul. At best, I imagined not ever having to think about them. I never considered the idea of being healed and whole from each and every one of them. But God healed all of them. He healed me, and I am not even triggered now. I didn't have to stuff the triggers away. He came and He healed them.

He is so gentle. He knew all along what triggered me. He knew why I was triggered every time even when it didn't make sense to me. He was never embarrassed when I got triggered. He was waiting for me to come to Him and ask Him why I got so triggered. He never brushed me away when I began to wonder with Him. He began to lead me to passages where His heart was revealed to me. I saw the Jesus of the Scriptures unlike the Jesus I grew up with in the darkness. I saw Jesus Christ of the Bible caring. He never mocked anyone when they wanted help, were hurting, or had questions pondering their pain. He listened. He took children up in His lap, and He loved them.

With each trigger I told Him about He gave me gifts. Safe gifts. He gave gifts for each alter inside when they told Him about the pain they lived through. He gave them gifts with their favorite colors of wrapping paper and ribbons on top to untie. The alters loved opening gifts from Him. They learned He was safe and He only gives good gifts to them. As I continued reading passages of truth in Scripture, I discovered His gifts. Each of them was unique to the situations shared with Him. They all included restoration, redemption, recompense, healing, and freedom with the gifts He gave.

He healed them with His love wrapped in these gifts. His healing balm for each trigger and memory as He talked to them personally was enough. He is the Great Physician and knew exactly what each one inside needed to heal. To this day, I am healed and free from all of the pain and torment and have no sting of any memory. His gifts of hope, life, and joy have healed all my places of pain with these memories.

Questions to Consider

1. What are you triggered by?

2. List each trigger and ask the Lord how He wants to heal them.

3. Write about various scriptures concerning truth about each trigger.

4. How does the Lord want to rid you of fear?

5. In reading scriptures about the gifts God gives, ask the Lord what gifts He desires to give you in your painful memories.

6. What gifts did the Lord send you from a person you knew?

7. What gift could you bring someone who is hurting to help him or her heal as the Lord leads?

Chapter 5

Moving forward from Memories

~∰◯

IN THE PROCESS of remembering horrific memories, it is normal for a hurting person to experience thoughts of denial. Denial can be a common theme in a person's life until her final stages of healing. It isn't unusual for her to think, *None of it really happened. I must be making all this up.* Denial acts to prevent us from seeing truth for what it is. This keeps us from experiencing the pain the truth may entail.

Also, it is very common for different alters to portray denial concerning memories of situations so they don't have to experience pain in those particular memories. I said earlier that alters are there to take the pain for the person. If this is true, why would different alters also have to experience denial to avoid the pain? Different alters serve different roles inside the person. A specific role that an alter may serve is to protect and deny the person from experiencing any pain. However, in doing this, they also keep the person from knowing what happened. When the Lord comes and ministers to each alter specifically, He takes the pain the alters have carried away. Then, the alter is free from her job and gets to integrate back into the wholeness of the person. The person is now able to know what memory the alter was carrying, and she is healed of any pain associated with the memory.

Emotions swirl inside of me. I don't want to cry. Pressure is building. Maybe I will cry. Nope. Visions of vivid memories occupy me.

When is he going to come back? I will have a lunch of ham and cheese sandwiches, milk in your tall red glass, cheese Doritos, and a large Snickers bar ready for you. You won't even have to take your work boots off first.

It never happened. He never did anything. The flannel shirts rubbed cozily up my cheeks, and I remember. We will die if we break the denial.

He took me canoeing, and we explored the wilderness where nature became our backyard. Days spent in the old truck together. He would whistle his tunes to the country songs playing on the radio station. I knew I had to hang on to those times. All other times of horror with him and the others must not be true. We had fun sometimes during the day. When I denied what he would do with me in darkness I died inside.

Nothing would change my perception of him until the voices inside my head became louder, when the dreams were coming to light during dark nights alone in my bed. Even when he died so suddenly I never cried. It was never safe inside for me to do so; my emotions were shut down. I didn't allow myself to shed a tear of grief. I was adamantly fine and became irritated when others questioned me otherwise with "How are you really doing?" questions. I wanted to forget it all.

I didn't even want to look at the good memories inside my head, as they were quickly becoming clouded by alters inside. They began to scream and wail from what was true. The alters also helped me ignore the memories they held. I was not in a place to receive what pain they held in my mind. It was the Lord's grace not allowing me to bear more than I could handle.

I was in the counseling office where the pictures of sailboats and sand dunes were impeccably placed on the walls to make it a more comfortable atmosphere. The lady with shoulder-length dirty blonde hair kept asking questions about me. I didn't know how to answer. I stayed frozen. I was afraid.

I didn't want her to know the real reasons why I was sitting there on the loveseat in my blue overalls and Nike tennis shoes. The screams inside my head kept saying everything was fine. If I said anything about what was happening inside of me, she would think I was crazy. I didn't know if this lady was safe. I didn't ever think anyone would believe me if they heard the truth.

Every time I went back to see her, I kept hearing more threats of what would happen to me if I saw her again. She was another Christian counselor. She prayed with me at times, and I felt safer when she did but not safe enough to believe nothing would happen to me if I let anything "bad" out. I didn't know how to stop the demonic threats shouting against alters inside.

Some time later I began meeting with a small group involving others who also had Dissociative Identity Disorder and found denial was a common trait among all of us. We found it was easy to deny everything because if we didn't believe any of it was true, we could move on and live "normally." I found my healing process delayed when my denial continued. This is just what the enemy wanted: for me to deny it all so I couldn't move forward and deal with what the Lord was bringing to the surface for continued healing.

Denial can be strong right up until the final stages of healing. If I struggled with denial, it wasn't because nothing happened, but because it's typical in the process of healing from DID/SRA. Bringing denial to the Lord and asking Him to reveal the truth will help keep us from deception. Many times when abuse happens, the tracks of abuse are strategically covered so the abused person may be convinced to think nothing happened. Even though abuse did take place, circumstances surrounding the situation are all different. Abusers do this in an attempt to show that the victim is falsely creating abusive scenarios.

An alter may be done dealing with a particular issue or memory and integrate. This doesn't necessarily mean another alter is done dealing with similar issues. We often deal with issues in layers as we experience different levels of healing, progressing line upon line. The same concept is true with alters inside, unless the Lord decides to do sovereign healings. I always longed for sovereign healing, but that was rarely the case with my own healing. When He chose this way, it was wonderful. The evidence of the power of the Lord during those times still makes my head spin as trauma and memories instantly left. No pain or evidence of the enemy remained.

Most times in ministry sessions I had memories and trauma dealt with line upon line. These were times where a memory was completely exposed, yet there was no pain in remembering anymore. It didn't sting. He allowed me to walk with Him in each of those times of trauma without my going through the pain and horror again. He is so tender. He will not allow us to bear anything we cannot handle. This was certainly true as I experienced ministry and healing from Him. He longs for every alter to be healed and free. Each one holds a key to the person's complete healing. As you minister in healing, ask the Lord what He desires to heal in alters who surface. Oftentimes when they surface, various lies they have been told by the enemy are exposed.

Lie: I will never be able to say what really happened. I am bad and evil because of what I have done and what I was made to do. No one will ever believe me. There is no way out. I have to keep it all inside or they will kill me.

Truth: "From my distress I called upon the LORD; the LORD answered me and set me in a large place. The LORD is for me; I will not fear; what can man do to me? The LORD is for me among those who help me; therefore I will look with satisfaction on those who hate me" (Ps. 118:5–7).

Lie: There are no safe people. I can't trust anyone. No one hears me when I cry. I can't ever let the secrets out.

Truth: "On God my salvation and my glory rest; the rock of my strength, my refuge is in God. Trust in Him at all times, O people; pour out your heart before Him; God is a refuge for us" (Ps. 62:7–8).

A memory was often remembered but never talked about until the Lord let me find safe people and allowed me to tell what happened. During times I shared in a safe place with those God provided to help, I found the heart of Christ. Those who helped minister to my brokenness demonstrated responses that matched the heart of Jesus Christ. This reveals who the Lord is. He is loving and full of compassion and healing. During these times, alters were able to see glimpses of how He really felt about them and what happened. His heart was moved with compassion toward them, and there is never any shadow about Him.

As I was learning to open up and feel safe with particular people, I always felt I did something wrong if the person started crying during my telling. I never quite understood why someone would cry for me over what I shared. I thought what I was saying were normal experiences, just what happened all the time in my life. Those memories were not the desire of the Lord Jesus Christ for my life. Safe people grieved for me as the Good Shepherd also grieved for me during those times. I always thought emotions of any kind were bad.

When I realized the safe people were never going to intentionally hurt me, I became less afraid of their normal emotions. I wasn't scared anymore when they were crying about what happened to me. They began to ask the Lord to come and heal. Often they would pray, "Lord, You saw what my friend experienced. What do You have to say about that?" Or, "Lord, You know the wickedness that took place. What were You doing during that time?"

It was at this point I came to know the Lord as my defender and the God who was on my side. When I began to hear the responses from the Lord through the Holy Spirit revealing truth to me from His Word, my beliefs about whether or not He would protect and defend me changed.

In Scripture I would consistently read passages that showed an emotional Jesus getting upset and crying. I discovered He had a heart "moved" with compassion and got angry about wickedness taking place. I began to believe the truth that He has a heart for people to be rescued from their enemies. He wants everything that binds us released so we live completely free in Him. A different Jesus than the one I grew up with began to come to life to me. I ended up "firing" the Jesus I knew until that point. I embraced the true Lord Jesus Christ as the emotional, powerful, loving Jesus Christ who took great vengeance upon my enemies who longed to destroy me.

> Oh give us help against the adversary, for deliverance by man is in vain.
>
> —Psalm 108:12

"Had it not been the LORD who was on our side," Let Israel now say, "Had it not been the LORD who was on our side, when men rose up against us, then they would have swallowed us alive, when their anger was kindled against us; then the waters would have engulfed us, the stream would have swept over our soul; then the raging waters would have swept over our soul." Blessed be the LORD, who has not given us to be torn by their teeth. Our soul has escaped as a bird out of the snare of the trapper; the snare is broken and we have escaped. Our help is in the name of the LORD, who made heaven and earth.

—Psalm 124:1–8

Will I always be awful?
Is emotional healing a possibility, or just a nice phrase I won't ever know?
Will I ever be normal inside?
They roped me like a mummy so I won't ever tell.
What is it like to not have darkness inside?
Roped tight in this cage.
Will I be tied up forever?

As different parts wonder if healing will ever be possible, they may think it will never get better and life will always be horrific. As this goes on, it is helpful as a core person to record what the alters are thinking, feeling, and questioning. It may be difficult for them to express any kind of emotion as they experience these hard things. The journal entry following is by the core person.

What will it be like when I know how much intensity of emotion I need for any given situation? Like, if my drink spills, to not react angrily or with much intensity than if my teacher gave me a bad grade on something I worked really hard on. The feelings all seem a blur, mixed together. No one can know.

High priest feet crackle stairs as he comes down. He's a nice man with false teeth playing cards with me. Cards you can almost see through 'cause they been through some rummy games. He would always win. He laughed when he won.

I hear sounds of wood floors creaking. It's about to happen again. The footsteps are getting closer. I will think something safe like yellow Starburst wrappers.

When I look at the wrapper it helps me leave what is really happening and then I just watch, so I don't feel any feelings inside. I like yellow. Yellow helps me when darkness happens.

Hate deck of cards. I like fifty-two pick-up. Make him get on the ground and stay there forever looking for all those stupid cards. Maybe when his pearly whites fall out this time they stay gone forever so I don't have to hear him say anything more.

I don't want to hear or feel what makes me die more inside each time he plays his games with me. Take the diamonds and club my heart. I hate this suit I live in. I hate it all.

I know the goblet he carries holds stuff I have to drink. He is coming closer with splashes of darkness inside the cup. I know the priestess will be angry if I object.

I smell his scent getting closer. More away inside I hide so I am not there anymore. I see myself below and I don't have to feel now. I feel so smart 'cause he doesn't know. I feel nothing as I lock my eyes to yellow Starburst wrapper I keep inside my bed until it is all over.

So I can't ever tell of the reds and blues and purples inside: mixed palettes of confusion. So much doesn't make sense inside. The colors I see aren't safe.

The red colors I don't like. Black colors. They outline pictures of what lies inside of here. Don't want to color the pictures being outlined inside. Close my eyes until all I see is black; no light about what has happened because nothing really happened anyway.

No one will understand. Is the sound I heard of shattered glass only in my imagination among voices that echo freedom outside? I heard them. They were giggling a laugh that sounded happy. What is joy?

I must be dreaming again. It won't ever happen. The sound in my mind is only an illusion, nothing that will ever take place. The sound of shattering continues to ring in my ears, and I am caught wondering if I should continue to hope for such a glorious sound. Did I really hear it?

Everything is supposed to be in a continuum. The pendulum can swing back and bruise harder. The freeze-frames blurred. There's no clarity of what happened because I never want to see it.

What memories?

Like outlines of pictures about to be painted, memories become bold, defining something inside my own mind's paintings. Molly painted it blurrier. Nothing was clear. No pretty perspectives anymore.

The Lord healed all of the pictures in my mind. He took all the colors of darkness and turned each of them into colors of His light, revealing different aspects of who He really is. The scribbles the enemy made on the canvas of my life were completely restored by the Lord and His poignant paintings of who He thought I was. He painted pictures I had never dreamed. He painted colors on canvases in my soul I had never seen before: colors not of this earth. With each memory, He painted His healing in me. His pictures overwhelm me and still cause me to cry, not because I am sad, but because His heart of love and healing for me is so overwhelming. He is a good God.

Oftentimes His goodness would be revealed in dreams I had. I knew these dreams were from Him, as He was also rescuing and redeeming my night hours. No longer were nights horrific for me. They became times of expectancy of what He would show me during the night. They are times of total peace, no fear, and security of His protection over me. I am convinced now He never sleeps. Instead He sings over me in the night hours and fills my mind with dreams, revealing Himself to me in indescribable ways.

I will never forget one night in particular. I had another one of these dreams. I knew He was in the process of healing all my memories but didn't know how He would heal each one of them. He did. Earlier I shared from an alter's perspective about losing her baby. I didn't know how He would heal the grief and pain and horror of those memories. He did it in a dream. I dreamed I was packing to get ready to go overseas. I already had sunscreen, a camera, film, a mosquito net, and a few long rolled-up skirts in my suitcase. On top of my bed my closet had exploded with various options for clothing, and I was not sure what to take for the long trip in a hot place.

I didn't know exactly where I was going in my dream, but I knew I was scheduled to speak at a conference to women who had been through trauma. I kept thinking as I was packing, *I don't know why they asked me to speak during the hour slot they gave me to speak.* I honestly didn't believe I was qualified to say anything to these women who had been through trauma. I knew there must have been another more equipped than I to speak and be in closer proximity.

I told the Lord in my dream I thought He had the wrong girl to speak to them. I told Him I still had issues of trauma to be healed from. Right then He asked me if I wanted to be well. Surprised at His response, I said, "Of course." I still had vaccination shots to complete that day before leaving for the trip. In my dream I heard the Lord ask me to see a gynecologist to get checked, as I had never seen any doctor of that sort because of pain from my past. He asked me to see that doctor when I went to the clinic for the rest of my shots. "Lord, I don't know if that doctor will be available then, and I need to get in and out so I can finish packing."

He asked, "Would you try to see her?"

"OK," I responded. So I went to the clinic in my dream and got my shots and asked if there was a gyno doc around. The nurse looked at me funny and asked if there was a problem. I told her no, but I needed to make sure everything was fine, as I was long overdue to see that doctor.

The nurse got the doctor and she asked me what was going on. The exam took place and she left to let me get dressed again. As I was still on the exam table in the dream, ocean waves were crashing over my whole body. I didn't know if I was in the ocean or in the sterile exam room. The pure, cleansing water kept gushing over me and I knew the Lord was speaking His healing, cleansing waves over me. Each gush of cleansing washed me from all the painful memories I needed freedom from before traveling to speak to anyone. The waves continued crashing over my mind and my entire body. I knew I had been completely cleansed.

A bit overwhelmed, I got dressed and went home to finish packing. The pain I had in my heart from memories of each baby who was sacrificed was totally gone. I knew I had been healed. I knew then I was ready to go wherever the Lord had me to go to declare His love, cleansing, and healing to anyone in need. Then I awoke. The pain from those particular memories was completely gone following my dream.

Questions to Consider

1. Have you had dreams and wondered if they were from the Lord? Ask the Lord what He longs to show you in them, correlating with the Scriptures as He leads.

2. How has the Lord healed you of particularly painful memories?

3. How does the Lord long to redeem each painful memory?

4. In Psalms, David discusses how the Lord turned his mourning into dancing. Where are you in this process?

5. Ask the Lord what needs to happen for this truth to be reality in your heart.

6. What losses have caused your heart to mourn?

7. What would it be like for your heart to dance again?

Chapter 6

Steps of Healing for DID/SRA

~❦

FACING DISSOCIATION IN my own mind as a possibility insinuated that occurrences I kept hearing in my head from alters might be true. I didn't want to face them. As I continued through my healing process, I learned some of the steps of healing of a person with Dissociative Identity Disorder. When I first became familiar with these steps, it made more sense to me as to where I was in the healing process. I learned I really was moving forward even when it seemed my life was only getting worse. Seven different steps were presented to me by Lydia Discipleship Ministries.

Step One: I'm Going Crazy

This is when I wondered why I had several sets of clothes in the closet: little girl outfits on the same rack with business-related pantsuits, trendy outfits, holey jeans and brand-name shirts of several colors. None of the styles went together. I often remember looking for something for going to a movie or hanging out with friends on Friday night and trying to figure out how on earth the bags full of clothes from Express, Banana Republic, and Wal-Mart ended up on my floor in the closet.

I hadn't remembered going to any of those places to get clothes. I remember pulling them out, thinking, *Who got these? These are not mine.* The low-cut tops, the cashmere sweaters, and pants with jeweled belts that fit too tightly on my legs as though they were leggings were not something I would wear. I figured all I could do was take them back. I knew if I couldn't figure out how they got on my floor in the closet the least I could do was try to clean up after such occurrences and try to make the best of those scenarios. I was frustrated.

I went to many different customer service returns sections of stores more times than I would like to admit. The employees knew my face and my driver's license number by heart from writing it down on their return slips so many times. I was embarrassed. They always asked if there was anything wrong with the items. I would always respond, "No, it just wasn't what I was looking for." When I started to figure out what was really happening and how I ended up with them, I started saying, "It just wasn't her style." Notoriously, they wouldn't be my style but the stores didn't have to know that. They would have thought I was foolish if I had bought something that wasn't my style only to have to return it, so I made it sound like I must have bought them for someone else.

Many times this would happen, and I would find items at home and I didn't know where they had come from, who had bought them, or how they ended up at my place. The clothes still in the bags were the easiest to deal with. At least I knew where to return them, and the best scenario would be that I could exchange them without the receipts. Alters inside always threw the receipts away, so getting money back was never an option. It was more infuriating when I didn't know where the items had come from.

I spent Saturdays trying to guess where items had come from, going from store to store to see if they had the same item or something comparable. When they did, I would attempt to return the items at the store. I remember one day I was home from work as the confusion in my mind was too much and I couldn't function with what I was expected to do as a CNA (Certified Nurse Assistant). The voices in my head were so loud that day, and the demonic forces were also influencing my thoughts. All I knew to do to make them stop was to try to numb them somehow or make myself go somewhere else so I didn't have to live it anymore.

I remember lying down on the floor, not knowing what else to do. I didn't want to get up again. I just cried and cried, begging God, if He was really there, to make my life go away because I couldn't live like this anymore. The next thing I knew, there was a boxing bag, which was not there before, all set up in my living room with boxing gloves nearby. The tool kit I didn't remember having was next to the gloves with the screwdriver and wrench still on the floor.

I knew an alter had been busy the last couple of hours. I didn't know where the items came from. No receipt of any kind was anywhere. I was trying to remember if the tool kit was something I really owned, or if it was also something I needed to return because I knew I couldn't keep this large Everlast stand and boxing bag. Not only did I not have the room for them, I knew they were expensive. I didn't even want to think about how to take it apart to take it back.

I looked around my apartment, and no boxes for an Everlast punching bag and stand were anywhere to be found. I got my slippers on and checked to see if they got thrown in the dumpster. Sure enough, long Everlast boxes were on top of everything else in the dumpster. Now, how I was going to get to them was something else. I had to go back to my apartment and get a step stool to try to see if I could reach the top of the dumpster to retrieve the boxes. No such luck. My stepstool never felt so short and I so foolish.

I must have looked helpless a few moments later as I realized I couldn't reach the boxes. A guy walking toward the dumpster asked if I needed help. I told him I could use more help than he could probably give, but I needed to get the boxes out to pack up an Everlast punching bag and stand to return to the store. He told me he had a ladder and that maybe that would be enough to get the boxes versus my step stool. I couldn't believe he was going to help me get them out.

As I waited for him to come back with the ladder I was overwhelmed with the Lord's provision. Every time I need help, the Lord always sees, and He either helps me or sends someone to help me. He saw me in my struggles when I thought there was no hope for me to live a normal life. The guy came with his red ladder, banged it up against the dumpster, climbed up, grabbed the boxes, and delicately tossed them to me. We gathered them. I was going to take them to my apartment when he asked if I needed help packing up the boxing bag and stand. I couldn't believe he was willing to help me to such an extent.

I suddenly felt a bit of fear, thinking he must have another agenda, because no one would really be willing to help me with that also. I told him I could probably pack them on my own and thanked him for his help. I took the boxes to my apartment and got busy disassembling the equipment and put them in the boxes with the last of my strapping tape to hold it together. I didn't know how I was going to get them to my car. They were too heavy for me to carry, and I didn't want to drag them down the stairs because I was afraid the boxes would come apart and the equipment would be damaged. Then I was sure to get no kind of exchange for returning them.

I started bringing down the boxing gloves in their smaller packaging to my car when I heard a guy from a balcony on the apartment asking if I needed to take it all to my car. It was the same guy who helped me get the boxes. Why he was on the balcony and saw me go to my car was a mystery to me. Then I wondered if the Lord had him wait up there to watch because He knew I needed help getting the equipment to my car. I told the guy, "Yes, I need help getting the boxes full of the equipment to my car." This was an hour and a half later from when he helped me get the boxes from the dumpster because it took that long to disassemble and pack the boxes. I couldn't believe he was still asking if I needed help. He came outside my apartment door and helped me carry all the boxes down and load them into my car. I thanked him profusely and he left. After changing clothes again I went to the store.

I was so full of gratitude that He sent someone every time to help me get through the chaos in my life. I asked the employees to help me unload the equipment to return it. They graciously helped and gave me store credit because I had no receipt again. I was relieved the equipment was out of my apartment and back at the store. I was frustrated this was another purchase that overdrew my account. This was often the case when I didn't know who inside had gotten what or when.

Occurrences that happen during the day may seem unexplainable. Loss of time occurs, and one may be an expert at making excuses to try to figure out what happened during lost time. The person may have cuts, bruises, and gashes on her body she can't explain. She may feel like her mind is a Rolodex of personalities flipping through the day, and she can't grasp chaos in her mind as she tries to survive. The person may change clothes several times a day and go to various places according to who is out. Whatever alter is "out" is how the person lives her life. Later, as the person develops in the healing process, she learns the alters were designed to help her survive, and they carry the person's trauma. Now, each alter needs to be brought the truth of who they are and how much the Lord loves them. He wants to bring them back into the wholeness of the person's mind. This step happens later but is brought to your attention now to bring understanding as to how the alters often operate.

Step Two: You're Going Crazy

Someone suggested to me it might be DID that I was dealing with. Many times someone recognized emotional shattering had taken place in me. I wondered if I was just making this all up or if these memories really happened. One thing I found particularly helpful during this step was acknowledging to God that whatever was true, that is what I chose to believe. This gives the Lord access to continue to show us the truth as well as help guard against deception as the Holy Spirit leads us into all truth.

This step in my journey was one of the more difficult to walk through because I knew I couldn't hide my life anymore. I knew others were recognizing my life was chaotic, confusing, and extremely abnormal. It was embarrassing to have others notice my life and for me to not be able to fix what was wrong immediately. I hated having my life seen for what it was and to have other people see how I lived. I hated having others question what was going on if I couldn't make it better right then. I hated others seeing me in my mess with them not knowing how to respond because I was too much for them. I hated being too much to be friends with. I had a Rolodex of friends, but I didn't know how to relate to them on a normal level of friendship. I didn't know what to do when they realized I was not a normal functioning friend. I hated always being in crisis and friends always being the sounding board for how crazy my life was. I couldn't seem to ever realize the basis of what was so wrong inside.

It wasn't that any of my friends were not loving, caring, or constantly praying for me. I remember one friend always saying, "I have holes in the knees of my jeans because of you." I didn't really know what she meant until later when she said, "My prayer life has become upside down because of you. I am always praying because of you, what you are constantly in crisis with, and the war you have inside all the time." Honestly, I was offended at first. I thought, *Me, always in crisis? Constant crises are only for crazy people. Wars inside someone's mind are only for those who are in the psychiatric ward. That's not me.* But it was very much me. Later I realized how gracious she was. I was privileged to have a friend who prayed as she did, though I didn't always like the fact she saw my life for what it was. She confronted me many times to get counseling or some kind of help. She knew I needed it. I just didn't know who on earth I would go to regarding all the voices inside and the bondage in my life.

The in-between time of recognizing how badly I needed to get help but not knowing who to trust was a place where many lies about hope were manifested in me. I didn't believe I would ever get the help I needed. This is where the enemy took advantage of my mind to get me to believe that if I ever told what happened I would be killed or locked away. Knowing I needed help as others confronted me at this point was scary because I was fearful those who saw my life would lock me up. I couldn't hide my life anymore. Again, the Lord in all His mercy provided the ways of escape for me. This will be shared in more detail later.

Step Three: We're Going Crazy

This is the place where I became more aware of the alters inside and their separate voices. I was trying to sort out the voices in all the confusion. This particular time was also very frustrating, confusing, and scary, trying to understand all the chaos taking place inside.

This step came when I began to acknowledge alters inside. I recognized that though there were many of them, they took one side or the other regarding the darkness or light of truth. I realized most of them were part of the darkness. I realized the few that were part of the light were still caught in deception from the others inside. I realized how the demons were influencing my life and had programmed my mind to surrender to the enemy's control at every turn I took in my life.

As this was taking place, life didn't get easier. It got harder because the enemy knew he was about to start losing his grip on my life and the drastic hold he had on my mind. I believe the war inside my mind got worse because of this. I felt I was going crazy when truth would begin to enter my mind through Scripture, a meeting at a church, or through a believer, because it stirred up alters as never before. They were all reacting to the truth they were hearing, though they weren't receptive at this point. Their voices were louder than they ever were before. Also during this time I began to struggle with the demonic realm in a way I never had before. I thought the dreams of demonic activity I was constantly having were a figment of my imagination many times, except for the fact that I would often wake up with evidences of the demonic attacking me during the night. I knew people would just think I was crazy if I told them. I was so afraid of having to say what was really happening. As my cries for help from the Lord were answered and He handpicked people to bring into my life, my journey became the most difficult, as described briefly in the next step.

Step Four: We're Going Crazy All the Time

This is the most crucial place to understand as a person is working through this step. When a person is being triggered a lot, she may be dealing with suicide attempts and ideation. The most emotional upheaval is taking place, and this is often the most chaotic time for the hurting person. The transition between this step and the next was most difficult for me. During this step I realized I desperately needed help, but didn't know what to say about what was going on inside my mind. I attempted suicide during this time, believing I was hopeless and that God would never heal me. I didn't know if anyone would ever be safe or if I should even dare speak about the trauma I was experiencing and remembering. I was fearful that if anyone knew what I was wrestling with, they would just send me to the hospital and I would never be believed or helped at all.

Many unknowns as to whether healing would ever be a possibility, much less a reality, and how others would respond frightened me and kept me from saying anything for years. I secretly prayed if there was any hope or healing for me, God would begin to show me and direct my steps to exactly what I needed. I hope to shed light on how amazing and faithful He was and continues to be. He has answered my cries for healing and freedom. I never thought I would ever be writing about how He has truly healed my heart and mind. I never believed my life would be so dramatically different today than it was then. I am now compelled to share for the rest of my days that He is the Deliverer and Healer, and, *yes*, He has come to set the captives free.

As I began to believe there were safe people in the world, the Lord led me to those who were both equipped and willing to help me heal. This is where my healing began to get messy and difficult. I still wondered if there was hope in the midst of what I was exposed to in the darkness and the life I created in my attempt to survive. There were still many times when I struggled with despair, deception, awful memories, doubt, and unbelief about who God is and whether He could and would heal me. I didn't really trust the Lord to heal me completely, but I believed if He could heal me in any way I would be further down the road than where I was.

I praise God for the different people who were willing to dig deep into areas of my heart and mind and allow me to be honest before them and the Lord about memories in my life.

They asked difficult questions I didn't always want to answer. They challenged me in ways that offended my victim mentality many times. I often thought of not meeting with them anymore and trying to pull myself up by my own bootstraps. At times, the truth they were challenging me with seemed painful. They never gave me anything but grace and mercy when I made bad decisions out of fear. They walked the road with me, interlocking their shields of faith that I would one day be whole because this was God's heart for me. They battled the darkness against me. They battled on my behalf, gave me tools to begin to battle, and reminded me the Lord is the One who fights for me.

I learned how much effectiveness I had in my own process. I learned I wasn't designed to discover freedom in my passivity, but to rise up and fight on my own behalf and discover my own freedom. This process took time. It was no overnight deal. I fought at times and cried, whined, and invited people to my pity party other times. But they didn't come. I was the only one at my pity parties, and I didn't obtain the freedom or healing I longed for during those times. I was frustrated frequently. I was mad at myself that I wasn't healed faster. I came to a place where I realized I needed to do whatever it took to be totally free, because this was no life to have. I was ready to be whole in spite of how difficult or painful it would be. I was ready for everything to be exposed so healing could come.

This was a huge shift in my freedom process, and I started to reach out to the different people who were helping me. I discovered there was help. I learned I wasn't crazy, but very broken. I discovered I wasn't hopeless, but He had a destiny of wholeness I had never dreamed of before. As I began to open what was inside, I discovered others could help me not go crazy anymore.

Step Five: Let Me Help You Not Go Crazy

This is when the core person takes on a new role in helping alters inside, acting as a "counselor" when they are stirred up and having difficulty. The person begins to assist the alters to find "new jobs" such as being a reporter of something taking place. This is a significant place for the core person to not just know truth in her head, but to begin to speak truth to alters inside. Not only does this reinforce the truth for the core person, but it also begins to marinate for alters to absorb until their full healing culminates to integration.

This is when I discovered freedom could be reality in my life. I learned I had the authority in Jesus Christ to help alters inside. I learned I could minister effectively to them by speaking truth to them in a way they understood. I could share scriptures with them. I could sing songs of life, peace, and love over them they hadn't known before. I could take authority over my thoughts. I could act as a referee to the alters who were fighting to hang on and to those who were sabotaging works of the Lord. I was grateful for the ways the alters lived life for me when I couldn't. It was no longer a time for them to sabotage, because the Lord was going to be the only One allowed to intervene from that point on. Only He would sabotage the darkness, not them. They were not darkness. They were precious to Him. He loved them. But the darkness they held on to was going to be sabotaged, and they would no longer be able to hold on unless they allowed the Lord to come in and rescue them. They were upset. They didn't like the idea of someone else coming in and messing things up inside.

It took months and months of this process to allow alters inside to see Jesus Christ of Nazareth was really safe and wanted the best for them. I allowed them to have all the time they needed when I saw how crucial this was in my healing. Though I didn't like the chaos that remained during these months, I knew it was necessary for them to be able to embrace Him, His truth, and ultimately surrender to Him so we could walk in wholeness.

Step Six: I'm Not Going Crazy as Often

This is when a person experiences fewer triggers, and when alters become more and more saturated and changed by truth. This is when I began to let go of the painful places. This is a place where the person may experience more stability in her healing, and is a calmer place inside as she continues to move forward.

I saw the greatest shift in my healing process during this time. This was the step that I was most excited to walk through as I began to notice dramatic changes He had done in my mind and heart. Before, I never believed this would be a reality. He began to show me how my life was in this step versus how my life used to be. I wrote a tremendous amount in journals in this process. I was in gratitude and awe of what was taking place and with the transitions the alters were engaging with. Life inside my mind was not the same. The alters were also trying to figure out how to operate without others to heckle them to darkness or without all of the demonic influences in my mind. Whole groups of alters began to be brought into my wholeness in this step. It was often a line-by-line process of individual alters inside being brought into the wholeness of my mind. Transitions of healing in greater measures also occurred during this time.

Step Seven: I Remember When I Used to Go Crazy

This was where my emotional stability and spiritual freedom were most active and evident, reflecting the measure of my healing. A person's mind becomes whole and there are no more fragments of different alters. The person understands and walks in the truth of her identity in Christ and in the fullness of who she was intended to be in the Kingdom of Light. She activates the belief the Lord had a destiny for her before the foundations of the world were created. The person understands and walks in her spiritual gifts and the gifts the Lord has naturally instilled. She realizes this is part of what makes her unique to fulfill the calling the Lord has specifically placed on her life.

This is where healing is no longer an unattainable goal for the hurting person, but her goal shifts. Now her goal is knowing Him and living the life to which He has called her. The paradigm shift of thinking life is all about me, to thinking my life was intended to live for Him changed the way I lived. I discovered His love, how drastic and real it was. His love ruined my lies of deserving a life of horror. I began to get excited about making it through the night. I began to look forward to getting up the next morning because He had ordained that day for me in His book before that day came to be. When I saw those truths like I was never able to see them before, I knew change and healing had taken place. I had never been so amazed healing had really happened in my mind like it had. I hope I never get over how powerful and loving He was and how His healing changed me to live life for Him in whatever capacity He has.

Questions to Consider

1. As a helper, ask the Lord if there are strongholds in your life. Ask Him to remove any distortions in hearing Him.

2. If the Lord speaks to you, ask Him how He wants to heal you and set you free. He desires freedom and wholeness in all of us.

3. According to Psalm 55:18, the Lord ransoms us unharmed from the battle waged against us, even though many oppose us. How have you seen the Lord ransom you unharmed in the battles you face daily?

4. Psalm 22:19–21, 24 talks about how the Lord has rescued us from the mouth of lions and has come quickly to save us. How has He rescued you from mouths of lions (liars)? Name areas in your life where you saw the Lord come quickly to save you. Worship Him for those times He came quickly to deliver you.

5. Psalm 107:16 declares that the Lord breaks down the gates of bronze and cuts the bars of iron. What areas in your life seem as bars of iron?

6. Ask the Lord to make this promise from Him reality in your life.

7. What changes need to be made in your life for Him to have the most access to allow this to happen?

Chapter 7

Bombard the Battleground

LATER WE WILL discuss what you as a helper can do to help the hurting person in the area of taking every thought captive. I mention the mind's battleground here because it is such a major player in the confusion and chaos the hurting person experiences on a constant basis. As her mind is already so bombarded with various voices of the alters inside, they are also being filled with lies from the enemy that add to the confusion and torment. How can one help those with Dissociative Identity Disorder to engage with truth, the Word of God? Here we will discuss ways a helper can minister practically in a situation like this.

As you are talking with the person you can incorporate Scripture into your conversation without making it obvious, so the person is not unnecessarily triggered. For example, if the person shares she is afraid of her brother, a way you could incorporate Scripture into the situation may be saying something like "Won't it be nice when you are able to experience peace in your heart about this situation so you don't have to be afraid anymore? The Good Shepherd is concerned and wants to help you with situations that make you afraid." You could have verses stored in the back of your

71

mind concerning strongholds the person may struggle with the most. Examples of strongholds may be fear, anxiety, depression, self-hatred, lust, and suicide, to name a few.

As a helper, knowing the Word is significant as you minister to the hurting person. Using Scripture as a sword against the enemy and presenting these same truths in "safer packaging" can help make it easier for her to absorb. The goal is to help her to absorb the truth of God's Word in very simple ways, eliminating confusion she experiences. She already has enough confusion and chaos to deal with in her mind. We don't need to compound her confusion, especially concerning truth that Jesus Christ can free and heal her.

Another practical tool one can use is to write a short verse or paraphrase a verse on an index card. If the verse is too difficult to absorb verbatim or handle at that particular time, this can be an easier way to process truth. As you do this you can talk about what that verse says and why it may be important to her healing process. Discuss any confusion or thoughts she is thinking as she reads the verse. Allowing her to discover an aspect of God's character through meditating on a verse of truth is significant in understanding who He is. A good way to do this would be to have her ask the question, "What does this verse show me about God?" For example, take the verses in Psalm 18 or Psalm 91. Read through the passage several times and ask that question. You may come up with several examples. Reflection as to how His character appears in these verses is a great starting place to see His face in the Word. Follow this exercise; meditate on His character and who He is. Remember, He never changes nor does His character.

God "Shaloms" the Shattered

The Lord is always true to who He really is, never going against His own character. He continually brings His freedom and truth as the person learns He is safe and trustworthy. He is incredibly faithful in making His presence and character real and near to the hurting person.

He never goes too fast for the person and knows the frailty of trust she struggles with. When everyone may have previously betrayed her and caused her pain, the God who sees and hears it all meets her as she is. The Lord often speaks to her in unmistakable ways, having such gentleness and clarity in what He says. He completely understands the soul and mind of one who has been shattered. He often addresses her specifically in Scripture with words of comfort and hope.

Though it is extremely difficult for a hurting person to read Scriptures sometimes, snapshots of His promises, even a sentence of Scripture on a piece of paper, can begin to speak to her about who God is and how God really thinks of her. Very often a hurting person's perception about God and whether or not He cares at all for her is quite distorted from the truth. As helpers, unless we know the truth, we won't know a lie when we hear it. When a hurting person tells us her beliefs concerning who God is, we must be able to discern what truth is. We *must* know truth.

It is not unusual for those with DID to not be able to read the Bible or portions of Scripture without an incredible amount of opposition and turmoil inside of them. Often in the beginning of their healing, they may find it difficult to have anything to do with the Bible at all. It may even bother them to touch or look at the Bible. Desires to destroy the pages of the Bible may also be something they struggle with. It's important to remember there may be such intense opposition inside of them they have desires that may seem bizarre, but they exist for a reason. No one feels or behaves a certain way for absolutely no reason.

Some say there is controversy that such a hideous form of abuse, Satanic Ritual Abuse, exists. Many with DID will confirm there is no such controversy. Instead, they tell very similar accounts of their experiences independently of each other. Additionally, those in the legal field will verify such abusive acts have taken place. Sometimes they discover the evidence and aftermath after a ritual has taken place. Satanic Ritual Abuse is directly related to the supernatural and in direct opposition to God, who He is, and what He has done for us.

Therefore, those perpetrating the abuse do everything to get the victim to be completely terrified of anything that relates to God, His character, and what He has done for us. The enemy desires to destroy the hope the Lord gives and the identity He alone has for us. The perpetrators of SRA will do anything to cause the victim to be fearful of the truth concerning God, His people, and those in authority who could potentially be helpful in getting help she needs. In doing this, the abusers will also cause the victim to form more alters inside to be programmed to cater to the enemy's destructive plans for her and respond in ways the abusers demand.

The enemy wants to destroy the hope that God gives, the identity He has for us, and anything involving the Bible and His truth. Satan is also adamant to captivate anyone, especially those who are victims of abuse, to hate and counteract the truths of Scripture and mock that which God treasures. I believe the enemy is particularly keen on victims of Satanic Ritual Abuse because he is the darkness that capitalizes on the evil perpetrated on the victim. SRA specifically causes curses and strongholds in the person's life that other kinds of abuse don't intentionally instill. The enemy intends to takes full advantage of any open door to wound a person's life, and he seems to be more evident in one who's experienced SRA.

In SRA, the victim is forced to do things and have things done to her that are horrific. Even in this kind of horror that takes place on an everyday basis, the Lord has allowed the mind of a person to survive and endure by allowing it to split into various alter personalities. These alters, which the enemy takes advantage of, are how the person survived her memories. The alters take the horror of what is going on so the person doesn't have to live in the horror. She doesn't even remember the horror until it is time for her healing process to begin in His perfect timing.

The abusers will also cause the victim to develop alters specifically programmed to respond in certain ways to those abusing her so the abusers are never exposed. This programming is continually enforced by perpetual abuse in various ceremonies so the secrets are locked inside the person by alters. The enemy intends for the core person to never remember what took place and never deal with what happened so she can never heal. Every kind of alter can be totally healed, regardless of how they split. God cares about all of them and wants to heal every part of what happened to wound them.

When someone with Dissociative Identity Disorder has difficulty reading the Bible, often what is happening is the enemy and his evil spirits influence her by taking advantage of her alters and dominating them. When an alter is loyal to the abusers and the darkness of the enemy she is in bondage to, the enemy has some control over how those particular alters function. Another reason why reading the Bible may be difficult for someone with DID is because the abusers are opposed to God and anything that has to do with Him. They will use the Bible in their rituals in an extremely distorted manner, causing the person to believe the Bible is a joke, evil, and is only quoted during the ceremonies in horribly distorting ways to mock the Lord. Because I grew up believing this, I developed knowledge of Scripture. I also developed the belief that Scripture would never help me unless it was in the context of darkness.

It was very difficult for me to embrace the holiness and power of Scripture as being from God Himself and not something that was intended to mock Him and His children. Even today I still struggle with passages I grew up learning in the ceremonies, and

I still ask the Lord to redeem all of His truth in me. Often, the scriptures I struggle with are verses that have to do with blood and the significance of the work of Jesus Christ, because these verses were used in various ceremonies as a complete mockery. The enemy tries to force fear in the victim as this happens so she never discovers the true significance of what really happened when Jesus Christ chose to die for us.

This causes the victim to believe the true Jesus Christ may only want to hurt her, keep her trapped, and ask her to do things harmful to others and herself. The goal of the darkness is to get the victim to believe that Jesus Christ has no power and cannot help her. The enemy tries to convince her only those of darkness will help her as demonstrated in rituals. The victim believes she has to be forever loyal to these abusers or terrible things will happen. Rituals describing what bad things will happen are also demonstrated, and the hurting person is made to participate. She often gives allegiance to the enemy, as continuous threats and abuse take place if the victim ever considers escaping the enemy's trap. But God. The enemy's plans failed and were all defeated in my life. I discovered the life-changing significance of Jesus Christ being crucified on the cross for me. God rescued me from the snares of the enemy.

Another tactic of the enemy is to do everything he can to keep the victim from discovering the truth of God's Word, the Bible. If the enemy can keep her from this, much of his game is won. She will never know the freedom that could potentially take place in her life because of the work of Jesus Christ on the cross. If the enemy can keep the victim from discovering freedom and truth, she will never realize the bondage that keeps her and the deception that has dominated her thinking. The lies in having no hope and no escape out of horror will never be broken except for truth and freedom in Christ. When she never knows complete freedom is possible, the motivation and incentive to look for a way out decreases considerably. This is especially the case when death threats are in place if the victim begins breaking free. Such threats make it difficult to pursue believing there is freedom, truth, and an escape. There is a way out! He came to rescue me. Jesus Christ of Nazareth has come running toward you also and wants to set us all totally free!

When it comes to discovering a God who really cares for one who is shattered, it may be hard for a hurting person to grasp. Questions such as, "Where was He when _____ happened?" or "If God cared so much, why didn't He stop _____ from happening?" may be common themes in her accusations of who she believes He is. As a helper, it is important that you encourage the hurting person to ask the Lord those specific questions and other pressing questions churning in her heart. Encourage her that God loves honest questions and is never afraid to acknowledge and answer them.

Another lie a hurting person might believe is "If He cares about my questions, He would have prevented _____ from happening so I wouldn't have to ask now." If she believes this, the enemy has a heyday when the hurting person concludes God doesn't want to hear her or He wouldn't really listen to her. A lie is that if God really hears her, then He would have done something when she cried out to Him when the horror occurred. But because He didn't "do anything" it must mean He doesn't hear her and doesn't care.

The next few chapters will address a few specific strongholds typical for one healing from DID/SRA. I dealt with each of these and was healed from all of them. There may be others you have encountered or struggled with. I encourage you to seek the Lord about each of them, as He desires for you to be free in every area of your life.

The enemy lives to try to kill us. If he doesn't succeed in killing us, his next best thing is for us to wish we were dead, because he attempts to make life devastating for us. Hurting people are especially vulnerable to believe any thoughts we have must be true, regardless of their source. Our thoughts either come from our flesh, the enemy, or from the truth of God's Word. Keeping this in mind, the enemy will do everything he can to fill our minds with his lies. Every thought that comes from him is a lie, as he is the father of all lies. A hurting person may think she is trapped forever. This thought is a lie from the enemy, because he wants her to believe it is true so she will never find freedom.

However, unless the truth in Scripture is revealed to the hurting person, she will continue to believe she is trapped. She must come to know, absorb, and believe the truth, to walk out of bondage she lives in. This is where the truth of God's Word becomes crucial in setting her free. When she begins to see the difference between truth and lies in her thought life, the iron bars that hold her captive in her mind will be cut asunder by the Word of God itself.

As a helper, you can point out that some of her thoughts may be lies. As she begins to tell you what she is thinking, in her own deception she will think it is all true. You can encourage her to look more closely at what her thoughts are and where they may be coming from. This is an area that may need to be addressed frequently, as she may be completely unaware that what she believes may be based on lies. Otherwise, she will experience continual bondage in her mind according to what the enemy places in her mind; lies will become the thoughts that she has and believes.

Here are a few examples of learning how to walk through this process of warring against the thoughts that I constantly had in my mind. Alters also deal with this. Following is their perspective in learning how to take these thoughts captive and submitting to the truth of Jesus Christ.

Lies: I will be trapped forever. I will never be able to escape. I will be locked up inside and no one will ever understand or be able to get to me when I need help.

If I ever say anything to anyone they won't understand me. I really am alone. No one will ever be able to help me. I will always be trapped inside this cage. People may peer in, but they will soon turn away, because no one will ever be able to help. No one will ever want to see me like this. Will I ever be unleashed from these ropes wrapped around me?

Truth: "No man will be able to stand before you all the days of your life. Just as I have been with Moses, I will be with you; I will not fail you or forsake you" (Josh. 1:5).

The real Jesus, the one who hasn't hurt me yet, says He will provide a way of escape for me. He says that when He closes a door, He will open another with my best interest in mind. He says He knows what is best for me. He knows and sees everything. He sees the ropes tied around me in this cage and I am desperate to escape. He says He is with me inside here. I am never alone.

He says though people may see me for a moment and turn away, He will never turn away from me. He says He is not ashamed of me inside this cage that seems to magnify all my faults. He says He will help me and make a way out. I wonder when I will hear the sound of these ropes whipping off me.

If only things could be explained using words. I don't want to deal with any of this torment anymore. I try to avoid it and only find myself worse off than before. What am I supposed to do with all of these feelings? What do I do when I feel uncomfortable to express what's really going on? I think reality is I am going crazy.

Truth: "The steadfast of mind You will keep in perfect peace, because he trusts in You. Trust in the LORD forever, for in GOD the LORD, we have an everlasting Rock" (Isa. 26:3–4).

For the hurting person reading these pages, it is important to remember the chaos and confusion inside your mind won't always be like this. There is hope in the midst of mind noise and chaos that may have been inside as long as you can remember. There is a way out of all the confusion. I am so glad you have been able to read to this point so far. You are so brave, and I pray that you will continue to engage with what you are reading and processing.

Stronger voices would often come when truth began to stir and challenge me. I did not know how to acknowledge what had occurred according to alters inside of me. I often chose to ignore what they were telling me. I didn't want to hear it. I thought it was all made up inside of me.

I wrote about the locked-away place. Someone inside thought the locked-away place in my mind would be the only safe place. Other alters inside still didn't believe there was a safe place among other malicious voices.

> So the ransomed of the LORD will return and come with joyful shouting to Zion, and everlasting joy will be on their heads. They will obtain gladness and joy, and sorrow and sighing will flee away.
>
> —Isaiah 51:11

I didn't intentionally help these alters, because I believed if I acknowledged they were in any kind of danger from other alters or the demonic, I would be acknowledging I was having a problem. I would be acknowledging my life wasn't normal inside my mind. I didn't like looking at conversations in my mind that weren't my own thoughts. I didn't want to look at the idea that I had Dissociative Identity Disorder. I was convinced

I must be just having a difficult time spiritually. I didn't know why I couldn't function in daily life as I noticed others were. I was tormented in my mind.

Questions to Consider

1. What do you think about most?

2. Ask the Lord if there are patterns in your thinking that reveal difficulties or strongholds in your life.

3. How does one know the difference between one's thoughts and lies of the enemy?

4. What should you do when you recognize your thoughts don't line up to the truth of Jesus Christ?

5. How can you take those thoughts captive? What does this look like practically?

6. Why is it important to take your thoughts captive?

7. Ask the Lord for strategies to create fortresses of truth in your mind and heart.

Chapter 8

Stronghold: Intense Self-Hatred

INTENSE SELF-HATRED IS extremely common in a hurting person with DID/SRA. As the abuse took place she wasn't allowed to process the trauma. This can result in lies she believes as part of her abuse. Usually she believes the abuse she experienced was deserved. The enemy then feeds her more lies to hate herself because he tells her that is what she deserves.

The fifty cents we got this morning after he prostituted us is supposed to be saved in the piggy bank.

He said we didn't deserve any more than fifty cents. We have to keep saving for the ice cream cone. Maybe we can get sprinkles this time.

I don't like wearing the tights she makes us put on for church. I hate dresses.

I like overalls with the cartoons and water boots with the brown coat, makes me feel like a boy. That is what I am.

Worthless. I feel like a throw-away inside. It is better if people don't know I'm here. They won't like me.

The desire to self-abuse and to act out on the hatred the hurting person feels inside is also a common trait of one who has been emotionally shattered. Because the hurting person was never able to acknowledge her pain and hatred toward her abusers, she resorts to acting out the hate on herself. She hopes, as she abuses herself, the pain won't have as much pressure inside anymore. As hatred is expressed on her, she believes this is safer than acting it out upon anyone else.

Also, because the enemy is always involved with abuse, his lies, such as "It's all your fault, no one will believe you, and you deserved it," may be rooted in her heart as a result. As the hurting person then takes on the shame of the abuse being her own fault and tries to figure out what she did to deserve it, she may turn to believing lies. These lies may be that because she "deserved" the abuse, she also "deserves" any self-abuse she inflicts upon herself. Shame constantly rears its ugly head, causing the hurting person to believe that she is worthless. The lies may convince her that she is trash and deserves nothing better than to be treated as such.

Sometimes cutting or self-harm can be a form of nonverbal communication. As the hurting person has been driven to a life of silence concerning her pain, self-harm may be used to tell others she has pain inside. She may be living a life of fear, afraid to say anything, or more harm will take place inside of her. However, if she hurts herself it is a way to tell someone she is hurting without speaking.

The collection of razor blades from my pink plastic package is in continuous supply underneath my mattress for any convenient use. They are something I know I can default to. They relieve pressure I feel is going to explode inside me. I don't know how long the voices will scream inside my head to slice satanic symbols on my legs and hips underneath covers. I am confused and overwhelmed. Just need some relief from all the chaos. Purples and blues and reds and blacks swirl in my mind.

For I am afflicted and needy, and my heart is wounded
within me.

—Psalm 109:22

I'm sitting outside the office where People *magazines and daily
newspapers neatly lie inside baskets nearby my eggplant cushioned
chair. I hear the murmuring of nurses ushering patients one-by-one
into the doctor's hallway. How am I going to explain the marks on
my hips if she sees them? What excuse can I come up with if she
wants me to strip everything except for my underwear? I can't let
her see. I don't want her to know there's anything going on.*

*My long-sleeve blouse on top of my long-sleeve undershirt will
surely deter her from needing to check anything physically. After all,
it is winter. Need to dress in layers. Warm. I know she is going to
call me back soon. I just won't say anything. I will keep my answers
short. She doesn't need to know. Keep it short and sweet and get out
as fast as possible. Then no one will know. I can do whatever I want
to punish me however I need to be punished. Whatever relieves the
pain. Whatever I deserve. I can control that. When I control it, it
doesn't hurt as bad.*

"How old are you this year?"

"Fifteen."

"OK, I will need you to take off everything from the waist
up so I can get a good look at your heart. Let me check your
blood pressure. Can you roll up your sleeves?"

Maybe if I just roll them up once that will be enough.

"What happened here?" she asked.

The dreaded question. Talk about something else. "Do
you think I have a low blood pressure? How do I know by the
numbers if my pressure is good or bad?" The distraction of my
question deterred her from the fresh marks from the blades.
Whew. I wanted to do anything to feel like I stayed in control.

Hurry and get dressed. Wear the pants with zipper pockets so you can tuck the blade in the pants pocket without being worried about anyone else noticing.

I like how the red trickles and quiets this blaring head because I have told them to shut up, and they listen. It slowly runs down, gravity propelling it to my knee. A bit of pressure is released and it is better inside. Not so intense inside here.

Does anyone know the darkness inside here? Someone else can see it. Can someone see when my soul shattered? Maybe someone else will know what is happening. Would someone really listen? Would they care? Would red colors that trickle down my body say what I can't?

It is hurting again and I am afraid it will scar. Why does she keep doing this? I want to be beautiful but don't know how it will happen if she keeps using the blades and sharp fingernails and anything that cuts to harm. What is she doing?

I won't be as beautiful if it keeps happening. Have to stay pretty. I see myself against the cage. My face with ropes around it. White pure flesh needs to stay young and non-marked or blemished. But it keeps happening anyway.

I guess I am too young to make a difference of what I say inside, because no one listens. The marks still happen. Maybe these ones won't scar. Enough already. Don't they know the white flesh is supposed to stay pretty to be a good mommy of baby inside me?

Another form of self-abuse, eating disorders, may also be present as you work with hurting people. Like cutting, an eating disorder is often done silently and privately. However, when it is revealed, it may be an attempt to tell someone the hurt inside is too much. Eventually, the disorder gets out of control, an irony to the hurting person who may use it as a means to have control.

The footsteps coming into stalls of the girls' bathroom are getting louder. Crouching over the basin in the stall on the very end I wait for them to leave before I stick two fingers to the back of my throat again. I can't let them hear me getting rid of the cafeteria lunch of hamburger and cold fries mixed with milk.

The girls stop in for a bathroom break and brag of the boy they asked out, the new jeans they bought from a trendy department store, they have too many zits, and Maybelline isn't working as well as the Cover Girl they had before. They didn't hear or see me kneeling in the stall. What would they think? I couldn't let anyone know. After I knew the remainders of any food left in me were gone I went to my locker.

Once again I controlled what came inside of me and what came out of me. I was so proud of myself. This secret was mine to keep forever and could never be taken away. I controlled it. I loved being the only one to say what food stayed and left. I always won this battle. I welcomed the familiar, acidic taste in my mouth. I grabbed the gum I kept inside my locker to help rid the potency.

The war inside me continued. I was caught between the voices.

You should have done it one more time because then there wouldn't be anything left inside of your system.

Doing it again before you go home will be necessary in order for the voices to leave you alone and be quiet.

What are you doing? You are going to get kicked off the basketball team, because you won't be able to practice as hard anymore, and the coaches will notice soon if you don't stop!

Just forget anything happened.

Nothing bad will happen to you. We will keep you safe and take care of the body as long as you never say anything to anyone.

If you eat tonight you can't eat at all tomorrow or we will make you hurt inside the stomach.

At the party, only eat the bare minimum so no one will wonder anything. We can't make them think anything is going on. Then, as soon as you have the first chance you need to get rid of it all.

If you don't let food inside of you at all, we won't torment you.

You would never really tell us to leave, because we are your only friends who really know you. Everyone else will reject you once they know you aren't normal. We are the only ones who really love you.

After getting the gum out of my locker, I renewed the vow I wouldn't eat until the next day. The torment got worse, but I couldn't say anything. The arguing inside my head increased. I thought throwing up again would be a way to get rid of the torment. I wanted the arguing inside to stop. I thought they were bad inside of me. I wanted to get rid of them all whether they helped or not.

I was confused by all of them. I didn't know there was a mixture of both spirits and dissociated voices I was dealing with. I didn't know what to listen to anymore as they opposed each other. I didn't know who to choose when both sides would give me a verdict of what I had to do, or I would be killed. I didn't know what was necessary in order to not upset others inside.

I am learning about distortions like "I just need to get over it," concerning an issue and my related progress. My spirit is not convinced this is a distortion. This distortion can't possibly be a lie, because I still believe it is true. I still believe this because I still struggle with purging my food. If people knew, they would think I should be able to stop. If I can't, there is something wrong with me, and I need to be condemned and punished.

None of this is said, because I never talk about this with anyone. I believe I need to further hurt myself because I continue to struggle.

Not eating is a punishment to myself. I should be delivered from this but I am not. There must be something wrong with me. I must have done something bad, and that must be why I can't be completely free from this.

I can't let anyone think I am still struggling with this issue of eating or not eating, because I should be well past this and healed by now. After all, I have even encouraged and prayed with others on this issue; I can't let anyone know. This secret is still an ugly monster I deal with. Can't give my secret away. It is one of the only things I can hang on to.

You don't deserve to eat after opening your big mouth about the conflict you were having with them in the office. Since you opened your trap only to embarrass us, we vow to not eat. You don't deserve to eat now. So what if the organ growls inside? That is what you get after allowing such vulnerability of someone else knowing about us when we don't think she is safe. We are not eating now. If you decide to eat against our wishes, we will make sure you get rid of it.

In spite of food drawing my stomach's attention back from the interview, I remember what happened prior to my leaving the office with the beginnings of a conflict being resolved. I couldn't help feeling as though I had let the cat out of the bag. I didn't know how to backpedal. I didn't know how to take back my words indicating there was something to deal with. It had already been done.

My spirit knew it was a good thing. Alters inside were bantering now on how to retaliate from opening my mouth. They didn't want anyone to know. The solution they had was to promise again not to eat for the entire day. I believed it was what I deserved after toying with the idea about opening my mouth to begin with.

I shouldn't have said anything. Now I am in trouble. Now I will have to pay. I don't want to feel. I wouldn't have to feel it, and I could release it from my system. When it stays inside my system I feel it rotting me away, contaminating who I am.

What are you doing? I said I wanted a taco!

I told you over and over again what I wanted to eat, so the choice is not hard. There are more than one of us who want a taco. What is the problem? You said yesterday you wouldn't let us go hungry even if you were mad. What are you doing then? There you go betraying us again. All I wanted was something.

A piece of bread will do. What can I do to make it better so I can eat? I don't know how I messed up this time. Would it help if I only asked for something small?

Please give me something besides water.

Are you going to let us have cookies later if we promise to not let anyone know about this? We won't tell.

Cassie wants a doughnut.

Can we make a deal with you so we at least get *something*? We will try not to tell about this if you can let us eat something.

Tonight I am reminded how snug the dress I wore to Amy's wedding fit today. How disgusting it felt to have excess skin between me and the flowing material of roses. I tried the scale again this evening. I hate this rollercoaster ride. I want to be in control. If only it wasn't mine, then slashes upon wrists wouldn't look as gorgeous. I would rather starve with this ache inside than eat and feel anything.

When I feel, I can't control the battle. When I feel like I lose both ways, demonic forces invade my mind to envision coffins and sweet, sappy epitaphs. Will this pendulum swing in my body ever center itself? All I ever wanted to do was be okay with myself and allow this ache to die. Tonight the ache is knocking at my soul's door,

*shouting profanities and questioning why I want to talk again. I
can't handle the feelings it carries, the teardrops it leaks. No more.*

*The war continues. The cords of death still mummify me. The
sound rattles inside this cage. Hopefully, those on the outside have
no idea. Wouldn't want them to know how things were.*

Want to keep everything as normal as possible.
Keep cage shut so no one knows.
Ropes tied around me won't ever come off.
Have to keep secrets. Nope. No struggle here.
Will darkness around me tremble?

It is not unusual for a hurting person to struggle intensely
with each of these issues, nor is it unusual for alters inside
the person to struggle even though the core person may not.
Rather than looking at symptoms of a disease, as helpers, we
must be in prayer for what the real root issues are the alters
deal with. What is really causing them to behave the way
they are?

As a helper of someone who has alters that deal with
self-abuse, what are some things you could do as you discover
this about them? Keep in mind, much of their self-abuse is an
unspoken cry for help. While they physically destruct their body,
they hope to release confusion, pressure, and chaos inside.

When I was struggling with these issues and was fearful
of talking about them I had a friend say, "Hmm. It looks like
you have lost some weight." I was mad she knew and that my
attempts to hide my struggles were obviously ineffective. Before
that time, my friend had mentioned she never confronts anyone
about a particular situation unless she has first wept over the
person in prayer about what the issue is doing to that person.
After she weeps over the person in prayer, the Lord may or may
not release her to say something to them.

I remembered that conversation and wondered if she had really done that for me. It was more amazing to discover that yes, she had been weeping over my pain and what my behavior and pain were doing to me. I couldn't imagine anyone doing that. At this point I began to see how much she really loved me.

I bring this situation up because as a helper, it is sometimes tempting to rush in, confront, and "fix" whatever is wrong concerning the hurting person. Allow me to encourage you to begin fighting for the person on your knees. Perhaps the Holy Spirit may tap you on the shoulder to say something motivated by love later. First, be willing to ask the Lord how what the person is doing may be hurting her. Allow Him to break your heart over her pain.

Questions to Consider

1. Who are you in Christ? As you read Scripture, begin to look for passages revealing your significance in Christ and your value to Him. (*Search for Significance* by Robert McGee and *Who I Am in Christ* by Neil Anderson were helpful sources for me.)

2. What do you think the enemy would be adamant about? Attacking one's value or trying to convince someone he or she is not worthy of any kind of love?

3. What are the schemes of the enemy when he attacks these areas in someone's life?

4. What are ways you can fight back against the enemy's attempts to destroy someone in these areas?

5. How would your life be different if you believed how valued you are by the Lord?

6. How would your life change if you believed others had the same extravagant value to Christ?

7. Is there anything else the Lord wants to show you concerning the stronghold of self-hatred? If so, ask the Lord about those things specifically.

Chapter 9

Stronghold: Suicidal Obsessions

AN UNDERLYING THEME in a person who has experienced extreme emotional chaos and suffering is having a compelling desire to die. It is not uncommon to recognize constant thoughts in a hurting person related to wanting to die from the chaos she experiences inside. Sometimes it feels like a rollercoaster she is forced to ride. If she gets sick while she rides there are consequences. All she wants is to end the ride and get off the rollercoaster. She may think that in dying, she would have control back. She wouldn't have to feel what she has been desperately avoiding. For a time she may have been successful not feeling, but when the feelings surface again, they come with pain the person may not want to deal with. She may think it would be easier to stop the pain by leaving her life forever.

Where is there a permanent cemetery for my soul,
Where I can finally cry,
Where I can feel the ache and not the fear,
Where I can wail and scream the secrets,

Where I can escape and cause the voices to vanish,
Where my dreams can die because I can't ever live,
Where the memories of torture turn from me?

I was invited to go jam with a few others in the hotel. I can't.
I don't want them to know anything. It is all too much and won't
stop my desires to die. Overdrive temptations will take the gold
medals of these games. Maybe those screaming the loudest inside
will finally be happy.

> How long, O LORD? Will You forget me forever? How long
> will You hide Your face from me? How long shall I take
> counsel in my soul, having sorrow in my heart all the day?
> How long will my enemy be exalted over me? Consider and
> answer me, O LORD my God; enlighten my eyes, or I will sleep
> the sleep of death, and my enemy will say, "I have overcome
> him," and my adversaries will rejoice when I am shaken. But
> I have trusted in Your lovingkindness; my heart shall rejoice
> in Your salvation. I will sing to the LORD, because He has
> dealt bountifully with me.
>
> —Psalm 13:1–6

One of the strategies used against my suicidal struggles
was having safe people who supported me emotionally and
spiritually. As I constantly debated with thoughts of suicide,
it was helpful to remember truth spoken in my life. A lie and
strategy of the enemy is to get us to believe struggles need to be
kept secret. It is common for those with DID to have a difficult
time with suicidal thoughts. When this struggle is in the light,
we can begin to walk in truth concerning thoughts of suicide
and dismantle this stronghold.

People who supported me became a team for me. I could
call them when I thought about taking my life. There were
several people who have been a part of my journey to help me
heal and see me come into freedom. Not one was more vital

than another. They each had a role in my life. A few were those I called when I felt suicidal.

Another was my doctor, who was also a Spirit-filled believer who helped me numerous times in her office. I would often just cry for no obvious reason. She allowed me to see I was not well, but there was hope. I knew something obvious was different about her. I knew she cared about me, but I didn't know why.

She carried something different inside. Whenever I saw her, something inside of me hoped I could be normal again. I didn't want to die anymore when I left her office. She encouraged me to keep a journal about what was happening inside and to bring it with me when I saw her. She had me keep a food journal. She asked hard questions to answer honestly. She knew the answers before she asked. One time she asked me why I wanted to die. I didn't know what to tell her without having the floodgates of pain burst to the surface.

She asked me if I was being tormented inside my thoughts and what the voices were saying. I had never talked to her about them. I knew the Holy Spirit spoke to her when she treated her patients. Because of the severity of my thoughts of suicide, she had me try antidepressants, not to cure the thoughts of suicide, but to take the edge off of the intensity my brain experienced as serotonin levels seemed imbalanced. She encouraged me to see a counselor and find a safe church.

I found a Christian counselor who I was able to share struggles of suicidal thoughts with. This helped during the times I engaged in our sessions. However, I was still so broken I didn't realize where these thoughts were coming from. I hoped the counselor would fix me. When this didn't happen, I became more frustrated and doubted any counselor could help me or that I could be honest with them. She was a competent counselor with years of experience, but I wasn't willing or ready to acknowledge to anyone what was happening inside. I was still living in my home state, where much of the abuse had taken place.

The Lord knew I needed to physically break from all the darkness and abuse before He would have me engage in healing necessary for freedom. I didn't think I would ever get free from my tormented mind. I still tried to write in my journal about battles taking place inside. Journaling helped get the battles of voices somewhere other than my own head. I still didn't know truth about my thoughts and that my thoughts of suicide were lies of the enemy trying to kill me. When I moved from my home state, I emailed those who supported and encouraged me often.

One of the ways emailing became especially helpful was that I wrote what was happening during those times. I could be angry, upset, furious, sad, and so forth, and write about what I was feeling more easily than if I talked. I found oftentimes I froze when I talked, because I was afraid of verbally releasing emotions.

Another benefit from writing consistently was looking back at previous writings and observing patterns of pain and progress. Before, it would have been harder to see progress, because there was nothing to refer to months before when I dealt with the same issues. Writing allowed me to notice my life was changing for good.

Below are some examples of emails I wrote to give an idea of how this was helpful. With some people being long distance, this was a practical way to keep in closer contact. Perhaps such a tool will be helpful for you as a helper, or as a hurting person if you don't have anyone you know of who can help in close proximity.

I am meeting with Sasha and Kate again tomorrow from noon until two p.m. These last few days have been a whirlwind of pressure inside of me, begging to be released. In Psalms, David was delivered constantly from his enemies and from the desperation and despair he felt. I wonder if freedom will ever come. I must keep fighting. I am fighting myself to keep my hands off the weapon.

My whole life, I have believed in the lie that the only place to be home is buried six feet under. I wish I didn't feel this way. I feel excluded from truth, like freedom will come to everyone else but me. I feel like I am impossible and freedom laughs at me because I don't have it yet.

I am having fun in my poetry class, trying to put words together to represent what freedom would look like. I want to believe freedom is possible for me. I want life.

I went to my doctor today because I needed her to fill out a prescription for antidepressant pills. She asked how I was doing. I told her I didn't notice any difference. I refrained from saying I felt worse mentally and emotionally than a week ago. She said if I hadn't noticed any difference in three days, to up the dosage to two times a day.

I thought, great, if this medicine doesn't kick in, I must be unfixable because my dosage was already high. I don't want to take such a dosage. Am I hopeless without it? It upsets me all of this has ended up going this far. I never considered myself as depressed. There has never been a time in my life where I haven't thought about taking my life.

> For You have delivered my soul from death, indeed my feet from stumbling, so that I may walk before God in the light of the living.
>
> —Psalm 56:13

Sometimes I wish I could just skip sleep. I think I would actually get more rest without sleep. I may call if needed. These demonic influences are relentless. Oh for their tails to be kicked for the last time!

I believe no one will ever read or find this in my lifetime. What is the logic of thinking it is alright to trust someone to tell them your plans for wanting to die? That would be ridiculous. After all, I always heard life was a big game. What happens when I lose?

No tears will be shed on this end. People told me they were concerned about my passivity of mind. No passivity here. Mind quite alert and attuned to what is happening; got it all planned. Perhaps they were referring to lies believed. No sense in convincing me that there are lies to deal with when it's all true inside.

There is no day left here. Moon is waning and waxing and this will all be over soon. I promised because nobody's going to rescue me from my horror.

The fantasy of a life without wanting to die is merely a dream. The thoughts I have won't let me go. All I should have is a dry eye and the face of a porcelain doll with no existence, because I was never expected or wanted anyway. There's no reason to think differently.

> But You, O LORD, be not far off; O You my help, hasten to my assistance. Deliver my soul from the sword, my only life from the power of the dog. Save me from the lion's mouth.
> —Psalm 22:19–21

The Lord knows what we suffer. He has not despised or disdained our suffering. He has not hidden His face from us. Instead, He has listened to our cry for help. Times when we're at our lowest, wanting to die, is when He's completely aware and wants to rescue us. He sees. He knows what's happening inside of us. He hears the alters scream and cry in anguish over the memories we hold. Why doesn't He answer or rescue us sooner? Ask Him. He is not afraid of our questions. He wants us to ask Him. He wants to answer us during our difficult times. He is waiting in the wings to answer our deepest cries.

It's crucial we ask questions honestly and with emotions as they come. He longs to be found in our search for Him. Allow Him to defend Himself though His Word, through the Holy Spirit. Let Him answer for Himself why the horror happened.

Ask Him why other horror didn't happen to us but to those we were forced to watch. He will never turn His ear from us. He is waiting with anticipation for our next question.

Tell Him your thoughts, feelings, and desires to die. He knows. It is common for the darkness to be at work in a lust for suicide. Remember, the Lord has ultimately kept you alive to this point. Ask God to help you and continue to protect you from plans the enemy has against you. The enemy wants to kill and destroy you. If he is not successful, his next best agenda is to keep you captive. If you commit suicide, the enemy will have accomplished the evil he intends for you. Don't let the enemy accomplish any of his agendas over you. You have come so far. You have worked so hard to survive. Don't let those who had you so trapped win after all you have been through to get to this point in your journey. Joy, life, and freedom come as the Lord heals.

In my mind at the time, any attempt of suicide was rational. It made sense to me because there didn't ever seem to be any other way for permanent relief. I always felt so inferior or stupid whenever I struggled with it. I always thought whenever I told someone about it I was stupid in even telling, because I was defeating my own plans. Lies and distortions were so embedded in me. The lies projected themselves as truth in my mind and caused me to want to die. I had a very difficult time sorting out lies concerning my reasons to die.

I had no concept that my reasons to die were not a rational way of thinking, because those reasons or thoughts came from Satan, the father of lies. Of course Satan loves to disguise himself to get us to think that his thoughts placed in our minds are really our thoughts. The more he can get us to think thoughts such as *I don't deserve to live, I always deserved to die, I was never supposed to be here anyway, I am taking up too much space in being alive,* and so forth, the more he can control us to do what he would want to do with us—ultimately kill us.

Until I was able to absorb pieces of truth, I was not aware how much of what I believed and how I lived reflected against what I was learning. I started off with just a verse a day, trying to memorize it, and asked the Lord how this could heal me today. At first I felt like I wasn't hearing from the Lord because I didn't know if what I heard was from Him, or from my own mind trying to confuse me.

I started with Jeremiah 29:11 (NIV): "'I know the plans I have for you,' declares the LORD, plans to prosper you and not to harm you, plans to give you hope and a future." Each time I read this verse and carried it around, I had thoughts opposing this verse. I didn't know why they were so adamant. Thoughts like *Shred the card inside your pocket or we will hurt you; bad things will happen to you if you keep reading that; don't tell anyone what you are about to do; we will make sure that you go through with it this time.*

> You have seen it, O LORD, do not keep silent; O Lord, do not be far from me. Stir up Yourself, and awake to my right, and to my cause, my God and my Lord. Judge me, O LORD my God, according to Your righteousness, and do not let them rejoice over me.
>
> —Psalm 35:22–24

The truth is, God wanted me to live an abundant life. He will always provide a way of escape to me that will bring me life. "There is no temptation that has seized you except what is common to man. But God is faithful, He will provide a way of escape" (1 Cor. 10:13 author's paraphrase). God wanted to deliver me Himself as I allowed Him to heal me.

When we are being deceived by a lie, only the truth can set us free from deception and reveal what will always bring us healing and life. One of the jobs of the Holy Spirit is to lead us into all truth and to remind us of the things we have already heard from Him (John 14). When we have the Holy Spirit inside of us, He helps us understand what the truth is and the lies and deceptions that we are walking in. When we are being deceived we don't know that we are deceived. This is why it is so crucial to be aggressive in steeping our minds in truth and understanding the truth of the Word of God.

The Word of God will reveal the distortions we believe that need to be changed, as well as show us the truth that counteracts the lies. God's Word is complete truth. Anything that I read that disagreed with what I believed challenged my beliefs not based on truth, but a lie from the enemy.

I did not find much help in rehearsing the verses quoted above until I came to believe that suicide indeed was a scheme of the enemy over my life, because he wants nothing more than to kill, steal, and destroy me (John 10:10). I began to see that Satan was my enemy and he was the initiator of suicidal thoughts in my life. Suicide was also an enemy of mine, because those thoughts came from the enemy.

This shift in my thinking, realizing that suicide and related thoughts needed to be treated as my enemies, changed how I responded to those thoughts. Thus, verses that pertained to the Lord dealing with my enemies became useful in learning how to be spiritually aggressive against them.

Recognizing the author of suicidal thoughts gave me understanding of who my enemy really was, Satan himself. I began to use truth of Scripture as a weapon against those suicidal thoughts. They did not go away instantly. The progress became evident when the thoughts became less frequent, and the times between the crises were longer than before. In the meantime, truth was becoming engraved on the tablets of my heart, transforming how I think.

By this I know that You are pleased with me, because my enemy does not shout in triumph over me.
—Psalm 41:11

Sometimes having a plan to use consistently on a momentary, hourly, or daily basis will be helpful for someone who is battling, versus dealing with the struggle without anything in place to help her. Why do I bring up having a plan concerning thoughts of suicide? For the same reason: when one who is battling with suicidal thoughts has a plan when she is struggling, she will be more likely to get through her struggle versus one who has no plan at all when she gets to such a difficult place. What can a plan look like? Simple is best. Those hurting can't afford any more confusion and chaos. Make it something easy to remember and follow.

For the Hurting Person

Think of people you can trust and list them and their phone numbers on a sheet of paper. Maybe no one comes to your mind. Ask God to help you identify people you can begin to trust. Maybe you can think of only one person. That is a good start. The more safe people you have around you the better. It is good to get as much healthy support as you can get! When you are feeling suicidal call a person who is a safe person for you. Let's say you are really blessed and know ten safe people who you can talk with. The second time you are feeling suicidal call the second person on your list; and the third time, the third person on your list, and so on. Talk to them about what you are struggling with. If you are comfortable have them pray with you and encourage you. You are not alone in this process. Even if you have no one you think you can call, ask God to come and make Himself real to you during this time.

If you have no one to call and these thoughts keep persisting, call a suicide hotline in your area to get through the humps of this kind of thinking. It is alright to check yourself into a hospital if you feel as though you are an immediate danger to yourself. Even if it is just temporary hospitalization, you need to be safe during this difficult time. It is normal to have feelings of shame, embarrassment, and hopelessness; but the truth is that you have nothing to be ashamed of, absolutely nothing. This is a difficult time for you that will get better. There is hope and freedom for you. There really is. If you know people you can call, ask them if they could go to the hospital with you so it is not so intimidating. They can help support you through this process.

Something that can be difficult concerning suicidal thoughts in one with Dissociative Identity Disorder is how to keep her "suicide proof." Though one without DID may still struggle with suicide at various levels, he may manage better to know his house is free from lethal medications, firearms, and so forth to help him from making an immediate decision for suicide. Granted, he may still be able to obtain such means. However, if he is being accountable to not have those means, it can help deter the temptation.

However, one with DID may be completely set on getting help and not committing suicide, while alters may want to kill other alters inside, ultimately killing the person. The alters are not irrational, but the thoughts of suicide are irrational. This is because it is not rational thinking for someone who is living a healthy, normal life to want to take her own life.

For the Helper

If someone has DID, a helper needs to know that the person's struggle with suicide may be different from someone else who thinks about suicide. It may be more intense. Urgency, self-hatred, and intense opposition of the enemy against her may be more prevalent inside. Different alters may have different desires concerning suicide. Remind her as a helper that it won't always be like this. Encourage her. Tell her you are proud of her for being brave and telling you what she is dealing with. Remind her you are with her and pray for her. If she is on the Lord's side, remind her that the God who lives inside of her now is greater than the one who has tried to destroy her. Remind her that God hates the pain she has gone through and He is so sad she is struggling. He wants to help her heal.

If the hurting person is adamant about killing herself or an alter, or another alter is adamant about killing the body or another one inside, explain to them they are all one body. If they kill "one" they will also be killing the whole body. Oftentimes different alters inside aren't even aware they are part of the whole person. They may feel their world is just them and the spiritual opposition that surrounds them.

Sometimes if an alter is set on this kind of thinking she may be a protector part. This alter may be aware of a curse over the person that is about to come to pass. She may know an event the person is supposed to go to that this alter is trying to hinder. Perhaps the only way she knows to keep it from happening is to kill the person so she won't have to go through any more pain. This is common if there is a solstice, full moon, or high day in the occult realm.

During these days the enemy's supernatural activity is heightened. Talk to the alter and let her know nothing bad has to happen to the person. Help her understand you are here to help her. Explain to her the One who can help and protect her best is the Good Shepherd. Ask the alter what her relationship to the Good Shepherd is. She may not be aware that He is on her side and wants to make sure nothing bad happens also. Encourage her to ask the Good Shepherd what the best solution is. Watch how the Lord responds and prayerfully go from there.

Always seek the Lord as you are talking to any alter. Remember, we want to facilitate revelation from the Lord Himself to the alter and to the person. If talking to a "protector" alter doesn't seem to help, another suggestion during a suicidal period is to ask if there is any alter who wants to live.

Ask if there is an alter who does not want to die. Make friends with her. Talk with her. See if you can engage with her enough to get her to tell you if there is danger about to happen or if other alters are trying to cause their suicidal plans to flourish. Encourage alters inside for being so brave to help keep this person alive. They may be tired from the other alters fighting and attempting to kill the person. Encourage them that they are such a significant part of the person. Pray the Lord would give them incredible strength in their innermost being. Pray that the God of all comfort and peace would fill them and uphold them, as they may feel like David against Goliath.

Questions to Consider

1. What do you think of when you hear Jesus came to give us life and life more abundantly?

2. Begin to meditate on scriptures relating to the life and hope God has for you. Memorize them. Pray them. Ask the Lord what verses would help build fortresses of truth in this area.

3. What areas in your heart have died because of the enemy's destruction in your life? How does the Lord want to breathe life into those areas again?

4. During the night hours when it may be most difficult, prepare by having verses of truth next to you declaring life and hope. Pray, intentionally declaring the truth of His desire for life for you, even when you don't feel like it.

5. Commit your choice for life to the Lord. Tell someone your commitment to choose life. When the enemy may attempt to destroy and kill you, ask the Lord to show you how to wield the Sword of the Spirit. Raise your shield of faith to believe His truths in your darkest hours.

6. Ask the Lord to show you the significance of why you are alive. What is your destiny in Him? If the enemy has tried as hard as he has to defeat and destroy you, what is he afraid of? The Lord has destined you for mighty purposes. Begin to pursue what your purposes in Christ are.

7. Do not give up! The Lord has complete healing and freedom for you. Do not give up or quit before you discover the amazing life of wholeness and abundant life He has planned for you. It is worth all the wait and struggle. He will heal and set you free if you allow Him.

Chapter 10

Fighting with Fear

The LORD is my light and my salvation; whom shall I fear?
The LORD is the defense of my life; whom shall I dread? When
evildoers came upon me to devour my flesh, my adversaries
and my enemies, they stumbled and fell. Though a host
encamp against me, my heart will not fear; though war arise
against me, in spite of this I shall be confident.

—Psalm 27:1–3

FEAR SUFFOCATES THE soul and keeps it from spreading
out of its cocoon. Fear ropes the mind to the restricting lies
of hell. Fear demolishes dreams given by the Lord to dare to
walk in destiny. Fear makes fun of what God says is true. Fear
compromises and diminishes love. Fear mocks transparency. Fear
cripples one from daring to be genuine. Fear squashes hope to
believe life could be any different. Fear is the backbone of the
enemy.

The enemy is cloaked in fear and deception. He always
desires to cause a person to fear anything other than the Lord
Most High. The enemy will do everything to keep a person

from hope and belief in the only love and hope that can set her free. "Perfect love casts out fear" (1 John 4:18). Perhaps this is why it's imperative for one to know perfect love in God alone. When one draws near to the perfect love of God, God casts out fear the enemy longs to bind and lodge in our hearts.

I never recall a time in darkness where fear didn't have overarching control. The fear did what it was supposed to. Fear made me afraid to believe God. Fear was afraid of exposing the darkness inside me. I couldn't speak about the spiritual darkness behind my eyes. I was afraid to talk concerning the truth of my chaos. Fear was my closest companion. He dripped threats and curses if I were to ever betray him. He often influenced how I behaved. I ran from people when I felt threatened that fear would hurt me if I talked to someone safe. I refused rest and faith in exchange for raging fear. I traded truth for turmoil.

My soul was in a tug-of-war for who would win. Both the fear of my enemies and God's faithfulness were in a battle for my soul. Until I was free from fear, I always believed the enemy would be the fierce father of my soul forever. But God demolished my enemy. He is mighty. He became the Father of my soul, and I now call Him Papa. He rescued my heart from being afraid. Papa began to brand His truths in me. I began to believe His words of life, which annihilated every fear beckoning to bind me.

There were specific fears I had concerning getting free. I suspect there are others reading this who want healing who have similar fears in trying to obtain freedom and healing. I will address the main fears I had and how the Lord ministered to me during those times.

Fear of Abandonment, Rejection, and Betrayal

Betrayal, rejection, and abandonment seemed to be three peas in a pod in my life growing up. The enemy's tactic was to cement my heart during this time to keep me from believing anyone was safe. As long as I believed no one was safe, there would be no one to help me, and I would stay in bondage forever. This included believing God wasn't safe also, and the enemy went to great lengths for me to believe that extravagant lie. However, the plans of the Lord trump the wicked. The heart of the Lord was to rescue my heart from the pit of lies I lived in. Every time I had been abandoned, betrayed, or rejected, the Lord made redemption. Did He do it right then? Not always. Not even often. But He did rescue me eventually and in perfect timing. He had the power to do it suddenly, but He also knew my heart didn't have the capacity to be receptive to His sudden rescuing right then. My heart needed to know my Rescuer before I embraced His rescuing. I didn't trust God during the times I was being abandoned. I didn't believe what He said about Himself or me. I traded His truth for the enemy's lies in my life.

The Lord knew the fears of abandonment in my life, and He would minister to alters inside wrestling with these lies the most. I didn't let Him do this until I knew Him. He began to reveal Himself to them in ways no one else could have, because no one else knew the alters inside at this point. He would come to them in dreams and reveal truth about Himself. Several mornings when I would write I noticed that pages in my journal were filled with handwritings from the alters who had written about a dream encountering the Lord. I didn't think too much about them writing in the journal as they wrote often. The dreams they were having about the Lord struck me. Here is an example of this:

He was sewing satin pink toe shoes. He was getting the pink ribbons from the hems of His tapestries and drawing them down by the angels. They got the ribbon and were twirling it around and braiding my hair with them. They were dancing with them and worshipping with the satin pink ribbons when the Lord asked if I wanted to dance and not be afraid ever again. I wanted to dance. But all of heaven was already dancing with exquisite garments and dancing shoes. I had none.

He asked me if I wanted shoes to dance with and I told Him I did. I remember thinking I didn't know what size shoe I wore and was afraid the shoes He was going to give me wouldn't fit. He gave me perfect, brand-new ballet toe shoes that were also satin pink and told me to put them on. I did and, like Cinderella, they were the perfect size. No one would have known but Him. I danced for the first time ever, and He was the One who came and told me it was okay to dance.

> Say to those with anxious heart, "Take courage, fear not. Behold, your God will come with vengeance; the recompense of God will come, but He will save you." . . . Then the lame will leap like a deer.
> —Isaiah 35:4, 6a

I realized again that the Lord goes to whatever length is needed in order for His precious creation to be set free. I began to see how much He loved them because of the ways He would constantly show His heart just for them. Another time I came home from classes to be welcomed by a foot-long Tootsie Roll. I asked my roommate if she knew anything about it, and she said she thought I had left it for some reason. I didn't know why it was on the table among recent mail, napkins, and a few cups from the kitchen. I told my roommate I didn't even like Tootsie Rolls and didn't know why it was there. That night an alter inside began to tell what had happened to my roommate.

I wanted to know if He was real. I told God my favorite thing was Tootsie Rolls. I told Him I would only know if He was real if He knew me. I didn't want to know anyone else who didn't care about me. Then, the coolest thing happened! We came home and the biggest Tootsie Roll I had ever seen in my life was on the kitchen table. I knew He was real. I wondered then if He really did care about me. I began to change my mind about who I knew Him to be. I never met anyone else who cared to know what I liked.

He gave me roses. One time I woke up to an undeniable smell of roses. I wondered if my windows were open and the breeze of spring was wafting in the smell of flowers from nearby. But it seemed stronger. I went to the living room and found a dozen red roses on my table. Gorgeous red. I never had a dozen roses in my whole life. I kept smelling and smelling. I even wondered if I was dreaming because it seemed too good to be true, roses being on my table when no one had gotten any. Joy never bought any flowers, much less expensive roses, and none of us alters had bought the roses. I asked the Lord who they were from and He simply said, "I love you." I knew then they were from Him. I still couldn't believe roses would actually be from the Lord on my table. I must have been dreaming. I received a knock on the door five minutes later. I figured maybe they would know about the roses or how they got on my table. They inquired if I had a couple eggs to spare for their breakfast and suddenly said, "Oh, it smells like roses in here. So sweet. Did someone give you roses?" At her comment, I knew the roses were there, and it was no longer merely my imagination. She left with two eggs and I left with knowing beyond the shadow of any doubt He really does love me.

> Blessed be the LORD, because He has heard the voice of my supplication. The LORD is my strength and my shield; my heart trusts in Him, and I am helped; therefore my heart exults, and with my song I shall thank Him.
> —Psalm 28:6–7

I often wondered why the Lord would show me His love so specifically. God knew I needed great healing from lies telling me I was worthless and would never be loved. God knew the enemy had great stake in convincing me no one would ever care about me. God knew I needed His attention for help. He was my help. Only through Him was my soul helped and healed.

Fear That My Life Could Never Be Better

As the Lord continued to display His heart countless times in similar scenarios as described, my heart began to trust in this Jesus Christ. He was extravagant in how He deliberately made Himself known to me. He held nothing back. When I had doubts and fears He would come and smash them with His truth and words of life over me. He ministered to each one inside during these times.

> On the day I called, You answer me; You made me bold with strength in my soul.
>
> —Psalm 138:3

I feared I would never find the help and healing I needed. I cried out to the Lord when I realized He was real and on my side to help me be whole again. I knew my mind and heart were shattered. I didn't know how to get the help required for me to have only one voice inside my head, my own thoughts, instead of numerous voices inside. I feared if I told anyone what was happening in me I would get sent to a psychiatric ward forever and still not get help. I feared no one would understand or believe what I experienced and what was occurring inside my mind. A tactic of the enemy is to get us to confirm our beliefs if they are based on lies. The enemy continued to scheme circumstances into my life to get me to believe the lies even more so than before. I could always hear the accuser, my enemy, then saying,

"See, your fears are true. Look at what happens when you asked for help and no one can help you. They think you are crazy. You must be crazy. There is really no hope for you." I learned the enemy always lies! Always! The Lord in His sovereign grace allowed me to see truth. I found truth. The Lord has come to save and heal all my brokenness. He began to hone the way for the healing I needed. I was no longer afraid I would never be healed when He consistently brought person after person to help me in my journey. Each person was vital in my victory to have joy, life, and complete freedom in Christ alone.

The Lord brought me out of the slimy pits of lies. The enemy wanted to convince me in my fears there was no way out for me. The enemy tried to convince me I was an exception to the truth of Christ and His healing power, because I was so severely shattered inside. The enemy wanted me to believe no one could help me, not even God. The Lord is triumphant over all the enemy's lies. The Lord proved His heart was for me when He came to minister to alters individually. He came to convince me His love was exceptional for me. He loved them uniquely. The Lord came and revealed His help to me when He hasn't always helped others the same way. Perhaps I was an exception for Him to specifically show His heart for me. He was my help. The Lord totally transformed my truths and convinced me He would heal me if I allowed Him.

Fear That the Enemy Had Control over Me

I am a daughter of the Most High God. I belong to Jesus Christ alone. No longer does the enemy have authority over my mind, will, or emotions. When I chose to give my life to Jesus Christ and for His purposes alone, I intentionally stepped out of the kingdom of darkness into the Kingdom of Light. Therefore, I now belong to God. Only the Holy Spirit has authority over who I am and how I behave as I choose to walk in the Spirit and not in my flesh. When I choose to walk in the flesh, the enemy tries to put thoughts into my mind that he hopes I respond to, according to his schemes over me. I don't have to respond to the lies and thoughts the enemy places in my mind. The enemy no longer controls my mind and heart, and the demonic influences that lived among the voices inside are longer there. The One who set me free, the Lord Most High, has delivered me from them all.

When I believed the enemy had control or more power over God, I believed I would always be captive. If the enemy was right, what hope would there have been for me? The enemy wanted me to believe anything from him to get me to think I was hopeless and would be his captive forever working in the kingdom of darkness. I was his slave. I wished I was dead when I was the slave of the enemy. The enemy tried to convince me God did have power to help and heal, but that God would never help me. The enemy tried to tell me I would only belong to him, and there was no way out. The enemy told me God is mighty, but never more powerful than Satan, because God would never come for me. The enemy came for me, pursued me, and captured me. The enemy told me God would never do that for me. But God showed me truth.

> Behold, the Lord GOD will come with might, with His arm ruling for Him. Behold, His reward is with Him, and His recompense before Him.
>
> —Isaiah 40:10

> Do not fear, for I am with you; do not anxiously look about you, for I am your God. I will strengthen you, surely I will help you, surely I will uphold you with My righteous right hand.
>
> —Isaiah 41:10

I stand completely free today to tell you *He did*. The Lord Almighty came for me, pursued me, and captured my heart with His love. He showed Himself Victor in every memory that He has allowed me to walk through and be restored and healed of. The Lord Most High is the One who pursued me like none other. He caught my heart in a hundred pieces and put them all back together in the wholeness of my mind again. He came for me like a knight in shining armor to deliver me from the enemy of my soul. I am victorious because He came, He pursued, and He captured me into His Kingdom to be whole and free.

Questions to Consider

1. What fears have captivated you?

2. What lies is the enemy attempting to convince you of regarding your fears?

3. What is God's truth concerning the enemy's lies?

4. What is God's truth concerning your fears?

5. Build fortresses of truth concerning areas of fear in your life.

6. Ask the Lord where the enemy is attempting to sabotage you in fear and how these areas have strategic purposes in the Lord's Kingdom as you walk in truth.

7. Ask the Lord how He wants to free you from fear.

HELP FOR HELPERS

I pray these pages minister to those who are broken, but also to those who are ministering to those who are shattered. These next couple of chapters will be specifically written for those who help. Does this mean those who are hurting get to skip the next couple chapters? Stayed tuned to them. Keep reading, because they will give insight to you as to how you can help your helpers. As we are all in need of support and help to get through healing in our lives, it is important to recognize pitfalls to avoid that are a detriment to our healing.

Included in these chapters will be various experiences from the support team the Lord placed in my life during various points in my journey. One of the biggest pitfalls in helping someone is becoming isolated and not having any support or prayer in ministry to another person. Different fears helpers had will be discussed, as well as specific ways the Lord revealed Himself to them as they worked with DID/SRA.

One of the traits I noticed the most while trying to get well was fear from those who hadn't helped people like me before. I realized later part of this was because the helpers didn't want to cause any more damage in my life. They knew there was already much pain and they didn't want to contribute more pain by not helping me the "right way." As long as we are dependent on the Lord and listening to Him, He gives us His heart and wisdom to minister as He longs to heal. There is no right way other than Christ Himself healing them! Not one person healed me. Many people walked with me, prayed with me, listened to many of my memories, heard me confess and repent of sin, and ministered to me in times of deliverance and healing. But they didn't heal or free me. Only He did it. He was the One who healed me. He is the One responsible for the healing and freedom He gave me. It is not up to any one person to heal or free, but Christ Jesus Himself.

Chapter 11

Frequent Fears a Helper May Have

~♨◯

Fear of Being Deceived

THOUGH THIS IS a common fear a helper may have, there are several things to keep in mind as you journey with the hurting person. It is imperative we are grounded in truth and the Word and continually surround ourselves with good Christian friends who uphold us in prayer and accountability. Also, it is important to continually ask the Lord to reveal any open doors to the enemy in our life so they can be diligently and intentionally shut. Asking the Lord consistently to expose deception and any sin in our lives will be a paved path to guard against deception of the enemy and his destruction in our lives. Deception and fear are both schemes of the enemy to destroy us. The enemy would love to deceive us into thinking and believing any lie as long as it keeps us from fulfilling our God-given destiny in the Lord's Kingdom. If you are fearful as you minister to one who is hurting, be intentional about guarding your mind and your heart with truth about the Lord's perfect love as it casts out fear of the enemy. Be intentional about choosing and acting on truth over lies in insecure places in your heart and vulnerable territories. Pump in truth that will combat these lies specifically.

As far as being deceived with what the hurting person is telling you, a way to minimize that is to be careful not to suggest anything or lead the hurting person on into thinking that something happened when it may not have. For example, if the hurting person is telling you about a situation, some good suggestions would be, "What happened? What was it that upsets you? Do you know the Good Shepherd? What do you think about Jesus?" Often what she tells you may be difficult to hear, perhaps even hard to believe. I have known some helpers to pray silently when a part is sharing about a horrific event that the helper would only be a reflection of the Lord, that any awful memory would simply reflect back to the Lord and not have any kind of impact or residue on the helper.

Because of the nature of what goes on in Satanic Ritual Abuse, the hurting person is most likely struggling to share the event or memory. As part of her abuse in SRA, she has been made to swear vows to never tell what has happened to her or what she has done. She is given threats and made to go through ceremonies of torture if she exposes what happens in the darkness; oftentimes they are threats of being sacrificed.

The significance of the secrets being broken is crucial and spiritually groundbreaking for them to find freedom. As a result, something else that may really help her is for you to ensure that she is safe and that you are listening to what she is telling you. Let her see that you are trustworthy; don't just tell her you are safe, but let her see how you interact with others and interact with the Lord. Remind her that the Lord is her protector and that if He has allowed her to get this far in her healing process, He will not allow anything to happen beyond what she can bear. Remind her that even when she says scary things and tells you the awful memories that you love her just as much. Pray against any retaliation and backlash of the enemy against them. Remind her that you are there to help her as the Lord leads and that you only desire the absolute best for her.

Fear of Asking for Too Much Prayer from Others

Though helpers are becoming more and more involved in hurting people's lives, it seems that SRA is still misunderstood in many Christian circles. Perhaps you realize this more and more as you seek additional prayer for yourself and the hurting person you know. You are not alone in your desire to help. Perhaps you are feeling alone in the process, wondering where other help for this hurting person may be, as well as help for you to minister to her effectively. Pray and ask the Lord to bring you people who will be a part of this process with you.

Don't allow the enemy to isolate you or get you to believe that because you have more knowledge of what to do in other situations, you don't need anyone else to support you as you invest in the hurting person's life. Arrogance that we can minister by ourselves is another pitfall the enemy will use to ensnare. The enemy desires to destroy us and certainly doesn't want a hurting person helped. This is one way he may try to destroy both you and the hurting person.

First and foremost, guard against these pitfalls by asking the Lord before you get involved what role He would give you in this person's life. The Lord uses all kinds of people in the journey of healing. Though it may be tempting to feel proud that the Lord is using you in the person's journey, do not let the enemy allow you to become prideful because "you are the only one who understands" this person. The hurting person may even tell you this. The enemy would love to take advantage of you with these kinds of thoughts. Be careful not to overstep the boundaries the Lord has given you in her life. Gather a few believers around you, even if they are not completely aware of what exactly is going on with you and the hurting person. Ask the Lord to keep you accountable with your time with the hurting person, seeing that you do not get off balance with the long hours of ministering to her, numerous crises calls, and so forth.

Especially if you have a family, seek the Lord concerning how much time you should spend and how much you should be involved in this person's life. The enemy would love nothing more than for you not to seek the Lord about your part in this person's life—perhaps resulting in a destroyed marriage and family because you did not seek the Lord on these issues. Talk it over with your spouse and family, keeping confidentiality and appropriateness in mind. Ask the Lord what He would have you share with them as you discuss it with your family to keep you spiritually, emotionally, and physically healthy. Remember, the enemy is after you and your family also. Pray with your family about any attacks and schemes the enemy has against you, especially as you are ministering to the hurting, turning the tables on the enemy to allow the hurting to find wholeness and freedom in the Lord Jesus Christ.

It may seem that there is no one else around to help the hurting person "like you can." Perhaps this is true. More importantly, since prayer should be the backbone of anything a believer decides to step into, ask the Lord if there is someone else who should be filling a greater role in this person's life. Often it may be tempting to take over someone else's role in that person's life because we didn't automatically see them as available. At the same time, if there is someone who is called to have a greater role in this person's life, begin praying for that additional helper, even before you meet him or her.

Specific ways you can pray for the helpers are to pray against any fears they may have to be removed from their life so they are able to walk in the destiny that God has for them. Pray that anything the enemy has that hinders them from stepping into what they are to be doing would be removed from their lives. Pray they would be open to whatever God has for them. Pray they would have people who confirm the Word of God in their lives and that they would begin to surround them in the truth. Pray the Lord's direction for their lives, whatever that looks like.

Be careful not to be parked in someone else's parking space when it comes to the specific things He has for us to do. Maybe someone else hasn't come along to help this person because we are in their parking space for who God has for them at that time. This isn't to say that you don't have a role in this person's life. The key is to ask the Lord what specific role you are to have and how you would activate it most effectively.

Fear of Being Inadequate and Unqualified

As we continually seek the Lord, He will continue to lead us into all truth and freedom. Two of the best traits of a helper are feeling completely inadequate and unqualified for the journey ahead. Absolute dependence on the Lord is necessary. Without Him we can do nothing. He alone is our help in anything we pursue. A word of caution would be to guard against thoughts of, *I have been to ____ training concerning these issues and have worked with____ amount of people and have ____amount of experience. So, I don't need to rely on the Lord as much anymore now that I have all this wonderful knowledge of the intricacies of SRA and DID.* Remember in the Garden of Eden, the tree the enemy enticed Adam and Eve to take part of was the Tree of the Knowledge of Good and Evil. What would have happened if Adam and Eve had been content to only take part of the Tree of Life instead? Only the Lord knows this.

The point to remember is that without absolute dependence on the Lord, we have nothing to offer them that is different from what the world offers: information and knowledge but not life the Lord longs to give them in setting them free. What makes believers distinguished from the rest of the world and their helping tactics is the Holy Spirit residing in us that brings forth truth, life, and His help for this person. We must be dependent on the Lord ourselves as we help others.

Fear That You Will Lose the Trust of the Person and the Alters Inside

In ministering with anyone it is important to keep your rapport with the person by not sharing specific things outside of your conversations, unless you first obtain her permission. Because the hurting person's trust has been betrayed so many times before, confidentiality is crucial to her. Let's say you were not aware of this and accidentally betrayed the trust of an alter or the person herself. Does this mean that you can't help her anymore? No. What are some ways to respond to the person after this has taken place? After asking the Lord how to respond, prayer for the person to be receptive to the truth and good communication on your part will be key. The hurting person may not yet have the necessary skills to communicate in conflict, so let her learn from your example of what good communication looks like in a scenario such as this.

For example, let's say that the hurting person you are ministering to is upset because you have not called her this week. This hurting person has been suicidal and you have felt overwhelmed as to how best to minister because you feel alone in this process. The hurting person may be angry with you and express feelings of being upset with you in a way that is hurtful and potentially damaging to your relationship with her.

As a helper, you could approach this situation in a variety of ways. One way could be to respond reactively to the hurting person by being upset and taking offense as she yells and speaks badly of you. While this would not be a good start in handling a conflict with her, it is a way many people deal with conflict, while others react to avoid it and passively pretend as though the elephant in the room isn't there. Another way to handle such a conflict would be to affirm to the hurting person that it is her choice to be upset about what happened, and you are willing to talk with her about what happened, what you desire for the hurting person, and what has upset her even if it involves you. Do not live in the flesh and allow your spirit to take offense. Be mindful to live in the Spirit while you have potentially prickly conversations.

Why would this be helpful? It helps the hurting person to know she is allowed to feel negative emotions and that it's possible to be in conflict with someone and not have the relationship forever sabotaged as a result. Even though conflicts occur in relationships, reconciliation and restoration are possible with the help and mercy of the Lord. When conflict occurs, it doesn't mean that relationships are over or need to be cut off. So often this is what the hurting person is used to, even so much as to tell you, "I don't want you in my life ever again. You hurt me just like everyone else!" Many times this is how she is used to relationships ending—in conflict without any kind of resolution or restoration of relationships.

As a helper, something else you could do is what I call "slowing down the conflict." By this I mean to encourage the person to meet you in an environment that isn't busy, a place where you can both be calm and discuss what happened. Make it a priority to get the problem resolved before the Lord. Talk about it specifically. This is helpful because the hurting person is used to a busy, chaotic mind. Being in an environment that is intentionally slower and highlighting the issue will keep the hurting person from minimizing what took place or if it hurt her. She has minimized the trauma in her life for years. Not that this is necessarily trauma, but it teaches her that it is safe now to talk about what happened and not minimize events in her life anymore. This is part of it. Making resolving the conflict a priority will model to her that it is important to you to hear what she has to say, even when she is upset. Discuss ways you could both handle the same scenario in the future. Keep the boundaries you and the Lord have as far as what your role is in this person's life, and be willing to talk with her about solutions.

Fear of the Enemy's Attacks if You Get Involved in the Person's Life

This fear could be taken to two extremes. One extreme would be to not be mindful of anything the enemy could do because you are on the Lord's side. In believing this extreme, you believe you would not need to have to spend time in the Word, have the armor of God on, or have a consistent prayer life because you are in Christ, so the enemy and his schemes would never come against you. What could the enemy possibly have to do with you?

The other extreme is that because you are working with a hurting person who may be involved with the enemy and dealing with the supernatural more than you may be familiar with, you look for a demon behind every bush in your encounters with this person. You are constantly fearful of what may happen during your meetings with this person. You may be afraid since you have ministered to this person, the enemy is going to wreck your life and get you in bondage as well. Both extremes are unhealthy and unbiblical.

What is the place the Lord would have us in-between extremes? How can we be spiritually grounded? As Scripture tells us, the enemy is doing everything in his power to kill, steal, and destroy us all. We must be mindful and alert for the enemy's schemes over us but also confident and secure in our position and authority in Christ over the enemy. Satan is no match for the living God inside of us. The living God inside the believer and the combat against the evil realm is not a power encounter but an authority encounter. The enemy is under our feet as we continue to rise in our authority and identity in Christ. It is crucial to be walking with the Lord as much as you are able as a believer, but especially when ministering to someone. Allowing any known or unknown sin in your life will hinder your effectiveness as a helper, but more significantly allow the enemy to have access to cause destruction in your life. Sin causes a relationship with God to be hindered and stops up our ears to hear clearly from Him when He is speaking to us through His Word and through others. It is imperative to have people surrounding you in prayer regardless of whether you are ministering to others or not. One of the tactics of the enemy is fear. Of course the enemy would want us to be afraid of what he might do or could do if we follow the Lord's leading in ministering to the hurting. We need to embrace several truths about our authority and power over the enemy during times we are afraid.

> And these whom He predestined, He also called; and these whom He called, He also justified; and these whom He justified, He also glorified. What then shall we say to these things? If God is for us, who is against us?
> —Romans 8:30–31

> The God of peace will soon crush Satan under your feet.
> —Romans 16:20

> Oh give us help against the adversary, for deliverance by man is in vain. Through God we will do valiantly; and it is He who shall tread down our adversaries.
> —Psalm 108:12–13

A Helper's View of Supporting One with DID

I thought it would help the helpers to have insight in what it was like for several people who helped me. To give you a little background, one of these helpers knew nothing about

Dissociative Identity Disorder when we first met. We often met at church and had spent some time together outside of church doing fun things. I didn't know she would become a part of my own healing process and a great friend. Following is some of her insight as she became aware of DID and her reactions as she came to know me and alters inside.

One of the first experiences I had in dealing with DID was talking to an alter who was afraid of decorations in the church. I later learned that individual alters may have a host of issues that can influence them. One might wonder, *How would I know where to start if the alter just began telling me a smorgasbord of difficult things they are dealing with?*

I learned that a good place to start is with the issue the alter initially begins to talk about. The significance of this is developing trust with them, regardless of what they share with you. Even if an alter is just beginning to talk to you, it would be good because it demonstrates a level of trust. Even if the topic seems to be easy for them to discuss or a difficult thing for them to talk about, if they are talking about something with you, it is significant and trust is growing.

At first I felt inadequate and unqualified to help at all. What really helped me was the perspective in seeing the person as not one with many alters and getting all freaked out by it, but seeing each alter for themselves, as individuals. As I began to do this, I was able to get to know the alter and develop trust with them. I asked them about their likes and dislikes and continually let them see that I was someone safe. If an alter was a younger age, it was just like talking to someone who was that age.

I let them know how much I enjoyed being with them and talking to them. Usually, when an issue is resolved the person comes back, or you can ask to speak to the person again. The countenance of the person changed when I knew that it was an alter. The times I talked to an alter they didn't have eye contact with me, but when the person was back they always would. This is a way I knew that the person was back. There are other ways to know this as well. Eye contact isn't the only way.

The very first time I ever talked to an alter was when I was praying for Joy and all of a sudden an alter said, "That's not my name!" My reaction to this statement was, "Do I talk to Joy now or do I talk to this alter?" I was confused at first and wondered what was going on. What was I supposed to do? Initially, I was afraid and fearful just because I was confused. But I don't remember thinking that it was demonic. It was pretty obvious to me that it was an alter rather than the enemy inside. In either case, it helped to ask who it was by asking their name and how old they were. Fortunately, they were willing to share this.

It is important to remember that different alters are there for various reasons. Because of this, they also have different individual personalities and may respond to you according to their pain. An example I ran into concerning this situation happened when talking to Cassie, an alter, and I learned she had a sweeter tone in talking with me versus Julie, another alter, who seemed to swear up a storm in her anger. That was a bit shocking to me at first. But I just talked to her like any other alter. "Why are you angry?" I asked. But I learned to treat each alter just as you would any other person. I thought it was like dealing with people in general. People don't act angry just because, but something is underneath their anger. The same is true with any alter that expresses any sort of emotion.

With this particular one we broke different vows of suicide. There was a lot we dealt with as I talked with this alter. The different alters led the direction of the conversation most of the time. I asked the alter a question and different alters interrupted at times. Others wouldn't say anything about the issue where other alters wanted someone safe to talk to about the same issue. For example, let's say I was talking to Julie, an alter, and Cassie, another alter, interrupted. Cassie explains why Julie won't talk about something that Julie and I were just discussing. Once Cassie explained and was done with her interruption, I asked if I could talk to Julie again. Then Julie was upset because she thought Cassie was tattling on her for explaining what was happening with her. I told Julie that I understood why she would be upset and talked about those feelings with her as well as the situation we were talking about before.

In regard to each alter, it is important to remember that you are not talking with them merely to suddenly get the person to be "one person." It wasn't my goal to make them "no longer there." However, in talking to Julie, I sincerely cared about her and each of the alters inside. I learned that it was significant to get to know them individually, as though they weren't a part of Joy but were one person in themselves. They had different thoughts, feelings, likes, dislikes, different experiences, and areas of pain that had yet to be discovered by someone else.

Especially in the situation above, an important help you can do is emphasize the trust you have with the alter in asking, "Is it alright if I share this with another alter who is struggling with what you shared with me?" Let's say in "real life" if I have a friend who is going through a hard time and I ask for advice for that person, I would not reveal that the person I get the advice from is the one struggling with that issue. It's sort of like confidentiality. Keeping confidentiality with the different alters is just as crucial in nurturing the trust that is being developed.

A simple example of this is when I talked to the alter Cassie and she told me some of the things that she liked, such as the color pink. A bigger example of this is when I talked to the alter Julie and in talking to her we discussed that she was honest about her anger and feelings of hatred for herself. We talked about her being open and how she wanted and had tried to kill herself and the reasons why.

I often thought, *What is this? What have I gotten myself into?* I later learned to emphasize trust and to ask alters if it was alright to share with others inside what they shared with me. I always felt like I didn't know what I was doing, knew that I wasn't a counselor, and prayed that she would be able to find people more equipped than I to pray and minister. I knew that my role was just to be Joy's friend. Sometimes it was difficult to know when to engage with what the alters were saying and when to just try to be with the person and allow them to be the one having fun and being together, rather than alters inside dominating the time we had together. I knew she was early in her healing process as she missed time a lot and often seemed confused. Frequently she didn't know why she was where she was. I cared about her so much and knew that one day life would be different for her.

During these times when the hurting person asks the hard questions, as a helper it is perfectly normal not to have the answers. In fact, I have found that I don't need to feel like I have to know the answer even if this person never talks to me again. It is in these times we specifically ask the Lord to speak clearly about the situation to them. If they are afraid of the Lord and they do not want to ask God themselves, I may ask, "Is it alright if I ask the Lord to show you the answer to what you want to ask Him?" Then, depending on their response, I will proceed either way. Praying to ask the Lord to guard the hurting person from deception is also important.

Questions to Consider

1. Ask the Lord what He wants for you to have while ministering to others.

2. How can you guard against deception of the enemy as you pursue healing or minister to one who's hurting?

3. How is prayer effective in ministering to one who's hurting?

4. How do you perceive the Lord is interceding for you as you are a Barnabas for the broken?

5. What makes us adequate helpers?

6. What can we do when we feel attacked by the enemy while we are helping one who's hurting? What authority do we have over the enemy?

7. What boundaries need to be in place as you minister to the hurting in your life?

Chapter 12

When Wholeness Was Hindered

~❦~

UNFORTUNATELY, IT IS not uncommon for those who have experienced severe abuse to have bad experiences in the church. Many churches often go to the extreme in dealing with hurting people, thinking that every problem just needs to be dealt with in a spiritual deliverance manner. Other churches go to an extreme on the other end of the scale, believing the hurting person's issues have nothing at all to do with spiritual matters and need to be treated simply as a mental or physical problem. Either extreme is unhealthy and, when related to one hurting, can cause more damage than healing for the hurting person.

I remember I was attending a new church after moving to a different area. The church was having a special spiritual freedom conference over a two-day period. The guest speaker declared that every problem a person could have—depression, physical sickness, emotional brokenness, problems in a marriage, broken relationships, and so forth—were all strictly from the influence of evil spirits at work in our lives. The simple solution then was to get rid of the demons in a person's life, and then the problems would be gone.

I went to the conference hoping that I could be delivered from my hurt. I didn't necessarily know how to handle all of what was going on inside of me and was open to thinking that spiritual deliverance may be beneficial. I had previously experienced deliverance sessions regarding several issues but didn't believe it was effective because I was still broken and in bondage. So, I went with my friend, who was also my transportation, and sat in the third row of seven. I kept thinking after I sat down that I wanted to sit in the very back. Something about the whole thing seemed awkward and uncomfortable.

The speaker didn't have to speak very long before I was done listening. He began talking about people who he had ministered to previously and his success. He explained that once the spirits were commanded to leave a person's life, the person was completely set free with no continuing problems relating to what bothered them. He said that he had a 100 percent success rate; not one person had returned to him saying that their problem remained. They were instantly free from the hurt and the issue they were dealing with. I thought to myself, *Sure, you are a traveling minister. No one could contact you telling you that they were still having problems if they wanted to because you are unable to be reached.* I also wondered how much the hurting individuals may feel guilt if they were still experiencing difficulty after such a "successful deliverance," causing them to think that if they were still having such a hard time it must be their fault rather than the method or formula the minister used.

After I quit listening and became more and more discouraged, I couldn't help but hear him address what he believed about the "supposed Dissociative Identity Disorder." For some reason my ears perked up, hoping that maybe his response would encourage a person to believe that God acknowledges the shattering that occurs in our mind and in our soul. I was disappointed again to hear that the "truth" in every "multiple personality case" he has dealt with ended up to be strictly a spiritual issue, and they needed to be delivered from particular spirits who posed as different personalities. He said every personality or alter a person had was directly influenced and caused by spirits indwelling the person's soul, causing the person to be deceived into thinking that she had Dissociative Identity Disorder, rather than being tormented by spirits that gave her new personalities.

Of course this is not true, even psychologically speaking, much less spiritually speaking. After hearing him say this, alters inside of me were irate, and I immediately wanted to leave. He continued to talk about this and said that any alters that were revealed during deliverance needed to be treated as a spirit and cast out as such. The truth is, much damage in a person's life can occur in their healing if an alter is attempted to be cast out. I knew for sure at this point that I could not have them pray for me anymore because the alters were too afraid he would be mean to them, try to get rid of them, and say that I was crazy to believe that there was something more than a spiritual issue going on.

Also, when we place ourselves under someone by having them lay hands on us and pray over us, we become submissive to whatever that person would pray over us. With this in mind, I refused prayer from anyone on his ministry team, because I knew I did not want to submit to them and their authority in prayer when I so strongly disagreed with them.

Another statement that raised a red flag was when he said that we could know if a spiritual deliverance was effective when the person threw up in order for the demons to leave them. Unless the person threw up when she was prayed for, she did not believe that the spirit had really left her. After watching this man minister in this way for two hours, I was so frustrated and angry at what I saw. They were encouraging people to get rid of the demon themselves by throwing up; this was how they knew it was really gone. This is not how Jesus handled wicked spirits in His ministry with those influenced by the darkness. I knew in my own spirit that the way the speaker handled spiritual deliverance was not based on truth.

I remained there but chose to eventually sit on the floor in the back to avoid being asked if I was alright or if I had been prayed for. I didn't want to be prayed for at all anymore. I had to stay because my ride was still receiving ministry and I didn't want to hinder her in any way. I watched for a few hours. After everyone had left, my friend was still there.

The minister came over to me and asked me if I had received prayer. I said no. He asked if I wanted prayer and I again said no. He asked why. I told him I didn't agree with what he was saying. He wanted to make a deal with me that if he prayed for me and I ended up to not really be free, then I had lost nothing, but to allow him to pray for me expecting God to heal and set me free would make the difference. He was saying that the reason why I had not really been completely set free was because I didn't have enough faith. I walked away even more frustrated. He did not understand. I was confused but knew what he was saying was not true. I continued to pray and ask the Lord for His truth and for continued healing. The Lord was gracious and revealed deceptions that were being spoken in that meeting.

Throughout my reading and continued studying of the Scriptures, I found that it is only His truth that can deliver us from any kind of deception. I remember telling the Lord in complete frustration, "I don't understand how everything works in the spiritual realm. All I know is that I want to be healed and for You to set me free from what has been keeping me from living the life You have intended for me to live, freedom from that which binds me." I asked Him to specifically show me His truth concerning the confusion I had. I wanted to deal with deceptions and misunderstandings in spiritual warfare issues.

He continually led me to portions of Scripture that gave me hope for complete freedom and healing. He taught me to have such a dependence on His Word, because it alone brings the breath of life to us when it is so close to being snuffed out within us. Because His Word is His own words of life, they alone can heal. I began to develop such a hunger and a thirst for His Word during this time. Realizing it was life and healing by itself gave me a greater desire to commune with the One who ordained its pages.

> Then they cried out to the LORD in their trouble; He saved them out of their distresses. He sent His word and healed them, and delivered them from their destructions.
> —Psalm 107:19–20

> As for God, His way is blameless; the word of the LORD is tried; He is a shield to all who take refuge in Him.
> —Psalm 18:30

The other difficulty a hurting person may have in trying to receive help from a church is that the church may see the hurting person's issues of dissociation and spiritual confusion as strictly a mental problem and give no regard to what may be spiritually taking place in the hurting person's life. This can be just as frustrating to experience as a church may think the solution to the person's issues is solely deliverance. Neither perspective brings into account that healing involves both spiritual intervention as well as cognitive intervention with the understanding of what has taken place in the hurting person's mind (dissociation) as a result of her abuse.

It seems as though when a hurting person may be seeking and doesn't know who to go to in the church, the average church person who doesn't understand the hurting person may think that a mental institution, psychiatric hospital, and medication are what the hurting person needs. While this may become a part of her process as her journey unfolds, ignoring the spiritual needs of the hurting person and the ramifications of what is happening inside of her as a result of trauma can be potentially devastating. This is a crucial need in her healing process.

As I was undergoing my own healing, I also found myself in a psychiatric ward after attempting suicide. I didn't want to share anything about what was really going on inside of me there, as I was required to stay seventy-two hours. One of the first things that the nurses did was put me on psychiatric medications without giving any attention to the spiritual or emotional issues that I dealt with at that point. Their perspective was to treat me as though my issues were only mental and once the drugs kicked in, I should be "just fine." Of course when the three weeks of taking those various medications were over and there was no change in my thinking, the spiritual and emotional confusion got worse.

I didn't feel safe to talk to anyone. I believed the nurse: that my problems may just be in my head. I started to believe that maybe I was just "making it up," or "making a big deal out of nothing," or that "I was just going crazy." While believing these lies, it became apparent to me how much the enemy wanted to hide me from the truth of what was really taking place. The Lord in His grace began to bring people into my life, one by one, who would walk with me, safe people I could talk to. I began to discover the truth of what was happening inside.

It is yelling at me to be silent again 'cause the brown hymnal in front of me has a cross on it. Makes me want to leave. When will it stop yelling inside here?

When they speak their tongues over me they get excited and afraid and cry all at the same time. Feel trapped again. Can't tell them to stop praying. But someone please make them stop. I don't want that kind of power inside of me again, and the tongues are being spoken again and sounds the same as it did when bad things happened.

Someone make them stop. Can't trust them anymore. Should have listened to silencer. I knew I should have listened. Now I am in more trouble inside than before. Can't tell anyone now.

One-Size-Fits-All Mentality

The other side of the swinging pendulum represents extremities in how the church may deal with spiritual warfare and emotional healing. They may think there is no spiritual warfare taking place when a hurting person is dealing with temptations such as suicide or self-abusive behavior. Even other issues the hurting person may deal with, such as depression or memories she is working through, may be considered as only being in the person's mind and there's nothing spiritual taking place. Ruling out the potential for spiritual warfare issues as a factor in a person's healing is detrimental if spiritual and demonic activity is active in a person's life and not handled as such. When the spiritual aspects are ignored and treated only as psychological, the enemy's entanglement remains hidden and the person remains trapped.

This is why is it so crucial for helpers of hurting people to have a balanced view on spiritual warfare as well as understanding what may be happening emotionally and cognitively in a hurting person. Also, it is significant to allow the Lord to continue to teach us while working with hurting people, because one person will not be the same as another. Remembering that while some of the issues a hurting person is dealing with may be similar to another hurting person, the tools that are most effective are only tools. The One who has allowed us to learn how to use the tools is the One who also knows best what the hurting person needs. Maybe it is to pick up one tool and lay the others aside. Because one tool may be extremely helpful in working with one hurting person, it doesn't necessarily mean the same tool will be as helpful in walking alongside another hurting person.

We are all created uniquely and, as helpers, need to most rely on the Holy Spirit before proceeding to the toolbox and picking up the tool we are accustomed to using. As we learn to walk with the hurting, allow the Holy Spirit to give you discernment specific to that person and how He would have you most effectively walk with her. Ask the Lord to keep you from any one methodology when it comes to walking with hurting people but to be completely led by His leading in helping them.

For example, while discipling a hurting person who finds memory work with her counselor helpful in their time of healing, another hurting person may not be able to go through the memories she is having. While one method of working through the memories she is may be helpful in the healing process, it doesn't mean the same thing will be beneficial to someone else during her own healing.

Also, a hurting person's spiritual and church background is so important to understand as a helper. If the hurting person comes from a legalistic background and is not necessarily familiar with the charismatic tendencies of helping people via spiritual warfare and deliverance work, he or she may be very afraid and sensitive to a helper who knows of those beneficial tools. But that may not be what that hurting person needs at that point in time. This doesn't mean that spiritual warfare and deliverance are not aspects of her healing, but one must be sensitive to the hurting person and to the Holy Spirit as to how she should be ministered to. We don't want to frighten her or make her think she is less important because she does not receive the ministry we have in mind for her. Remember, the Lord is the One who heals and ministers to her.

As a helper, one must remember that all people are unique with individual needs as a person. While walking with a hurting person through her healing, our goal is to facilitate revelation.

Our focus is, by the operation of the Holy Spirit, to be able to place her hand and God's hand together, allowing the hurting person to receive the healing that comes only from the Lord Himself. More than a helper, the Lord desires to see the hurting whole, those held captive set free.

> The Spirit of the Lord GOD is upon me, because the LORD has anointed me to bring good news to the afflicted; He has sent me to bind up the brokenhearted, to proclaim liberty to captives and freedom to prisoners; to proclaim the favorable year of the LORD and the day of vengeance of our God; to comfort all who mourn, to grant those who mourn in Zion, giving them a garland instead of ashes, the oil of gladness instead of mourning, the mantle of praise instead of a spirit of fainting. So they will be called oaks of righteousness, the planting of the LORD, that He may be glorified.
> —Isaiah 61:1–3

The lady with the green shirt I like. Maybe she won't lay her hands on my shoulders like happened last time. Didn't like.

She has pink cheeks. Maybe one day I can wear the makeup too. I try not to be afraid when she talks to me about asking my "friends" to leave that live inside of me. But I don't want them to go yet. I don't want them to leave. I like my friends inside. They help me. They help me not go to the dirt hole where I will be forever if they leave.

Keep quiet about the dug hole.

Things must not be bad. I must be making up all the bad things that happen inside of my mind. Mind go away. Betraying mind goes against nice things I must remember.

Even though one person you are working with may have an alter that holds a memory of being in a hole and being rescued, it doesn't necessarily mean that all the people you are working with, though memories may be similar, will have the same memories or alters that operate in similar jobs.

For example, in the previous excerpt from an alter, her job in the person may be to help carry denial. By this, I mean that in order for the person to come to a point of realizing truth as it happened to her, the Lord must bring her to a place where she is in a safe enough environment physically, emotionally, and spiritually to acknowledge what she may have denied for years. Some of the reasons why the denial is so strong even up to the final stages of a person's healing may be if it happened, then other people will just think that she is crazy or making it all up. If it is really true, then the surrounding environment where the events took place would have made sense afterward. If it really happened, she must be a horrible person and must have deserved what happened to her. If it happened, it will be too painful to look at as truth and deal with. If it happened, then her whole life up to that point may be shattering the lie that she has been "successfully" living and that everything is fine.

The Lord is gracious in that He never brings the hurting person to a place of acknowledging a hard truth until she is able to handle the truth and its ramifications. When helping a person to face a truth about her past, another person who is facing a similar memory may be further along in her healing process than the first person. This may be because the Lord knows exactly what the first person can handle. In His perfect timing, He will bring the person to the truth. It will match support and grace that is sufficient for her. The other person may not come to a similar memory or truth as quickly as the first person because the Lord knows her and her needs exactly. He will work with that person individually and has a different plan for her healing that often may include a different time frame. It isn't that either one of the hurting people is growing faster than the other. They may both have hearts that desire complete healing and may both be aggressive in pursuing healing from the Lord, but the ultimate plan of their healing may look much different from each other as they work with those helping them.

As a helper of the hurting, one must remember to look to the Lord for discernment. Ask Him where He wants to take the hurting person individually as you work with her, and continue to place the hurting person's heart into the Lord's hands. As the hurting person learns to process truth, whether it is the truth of what happened in her past, or the truth of God's Word about her and/or the situation, one must be sensitive to where that person is emotionally and spiritually during this process. As this can be an extremely painful process emotionally, the person may not be ready to move to the next step in the healing process. As a helper it is more important to be focused on how the hurting person may be processing truth rather than an agenda of completing steps necessary for her healing.

As this process continues it may be easy to have the tendency to think that because the process has slowed down, the person is not being aggressive in her own healing anymore but becoming passive. As we rely on the Holy Spirit and continue to walk closely with the hurting person, this is where walking the process out is crucial. Though times of breakthrough and deliverance will come, the times in-between these mountaintops in a person's healing are really where the person learns to absorb and process the truth needed to break the lies embedded inside. As this takes place, freedom, as slow as it may seem at times, will come from the inside out, renewing her mind and emotions.

When we understand the character of God and who He is, we have a clearer perception of what He says when He speaks to us. Recently, I was praying about something, and I felt like He was directly speaking to me about it before anything happened concerning the issue. I thought I had heard Him but was so afraid that I heard Him wrong because I was struggling with Him speaking to me about something. So I acted as though I didn't hear Him speak to me. I just kept it inside my spirit and did not respond to Him about what He spoke to me.

God wants me to choose to believe the truth that He speaks to me. If He says that He promises to provide for me, He wants me to choose to believe that He will provide because that is what He has already spoken to me. By choosing and declaring this truth, the fertile soil in our minds will grow stronger in His truth.

Questions to Consider

1. Psalm 107:19–20 states, "Then they cried out to the LORD in their trouble; He saved them out of their distresses. He sent His word and healed them, and delivered them from their destructions." How has the Lord sent forth His Word in your life and healed you? What graves do you still need rescuing from?

2. Ask the Lord what He wants to show you concerning the significance of the armor of God, declaring the truth, wielding the Sword of the Spirit, walking in our authority in Christ, and ways to keep the enemy at bay in your life.

3. What is the difference between one who is speaking as an alter inside a hurting person versus a hurting person who is manifesting demonic influence?

4. As a helper, when you encounter an alter in someone with DID, what prayers may be beneficial to the hurting person and to you as you help her?

5. Psalm 18:30 says, "As for God, His way is blameless; the word of the LORD is tried; He is a shield to all who take refuge in Him." When have you found this to be reality in your own life? How has His Word shielded you? From what?

6. What are ways you can encourage a hurting person who is highly triggered by church and the common symbolisms that trigger her?

7. Begin to pray for those in your church leadership. Ask the Lord how He wants you to pray for them. How are you to walk alongside them as part of His Kingdom Church? Ask the Lord for forgiveness in any areas you have not been faithful to support them in prayer and in any practical ways He has spoken to you about. Ask the Lord if you need to go to them in repentance and walk in obedience.

WHAT HELPS HEALING ALONG?

These next chapters explain various aspects of what helped my healing process. One crucial element the Lord provided in my healing process was a ministry team around me. This was a supportive group of people the Lord strategically placed in my life at different points of progress. During the beginning of pursuing healing, the Lord was gracious to put different people in my life who were able to meet with me together and separately.

I was once told by one of my helpers that healing would be 10 percent meeting with them in ministry/prayer sessions, and the other 90 percent would be my own pursuit to set my face like flint to get free. I had no idea then that my decisions and my choices in how I lived life made the difference in whether or not I wanted my life to change. I didn't know how crucial it was to take my thoughts captive. I didn't know that taking my thoughts captive would be the difference in whether or not I had victory over an area I struggled with consistently. I didn't know the choices I could now make every day would be the difference between life and death for me. I didn't know I could make choices. I learned quickly I had been making choices all my life. However, the majority of the choices I made—even after I was forced to participate in darkness—were choices to believe my life would never be different. My choices even then influenced beliefs that I would be in bondage unless the Lord rescued me. He did and taught me I also had a huge role in my being rescued by what I set my mind on from that day forward.

Healing was 90 percent of choices I made, what I set my mind on, how I chose to spend time, and whether I listened to lies versus truth. I could have stayed in bondage, but healing required intentional decisions of change, choices, and surrender to Him to allow His truth to transform me.

Chapter 13

What Helps Healing Along?
A Supportive Ministry Team

~♫☙

DURING THE BEGINNING of my healing the Lord provided a team of people around me to support me. I didn't even know I wasn't ready for the deep healing needed to deal specifically with Satanic Ritual Abuse and Dissociative Identity Disorder. This wasn't dealt with specifically at this time. He knew that to prepare me for healing from SRA, this team was necessary in the beginning stages.

My problem was trying to figure out who was safest and who I could possibly ask to be a part of this team. Also, I had to determine what I would do if they rejected my asking. I was intimidated about asking anyone, though at that point I had a few people in mind. They didn't know the other people involved who were helping me. Coming together in a meeting would be a way for everyone to be on the same page in helping me find healing, knowing what I was struggling with, and making sure they knew occurrences from week to week.

The Lord developed a team of people around me, all serving different functions in the beginning stages of healing. It consisted of several people. Each had a unique relationship with the Lord and each met a different need concerning healing in my life. The team consisted of my roommate, who was also a good friend; my doctor, who was a Spirit-filled believer; a Christian counselor; a mentor who walked me through reading various Scripture passages; and a mentor who prayed with me when I had difficulties with darkness.

My counselor became a significant person in the stages of my healing. With her I discovered that things could be better for me inside. I really wanted to work at finding healing but didn't really know how. She suggested having a meeting with the people who I felt most safe with and discussing together how they could be the most helpful and supportive to me during this time.

My counselor became the facilitator and the first meeting consisted of my doctor, my discipler, and one who was leading me through spiritual warfare and prayed with me when I struggled. Though we didn't have many meetings, a good network was formed, and I felt like I could talk to them about some of what was bothering me once everyone was on the same page. My counselor seemed to understand DID and was the first to tell me she thought that my memories revealed a background I didn't want to face. She told me I would have difficulty receiving healing unless I was willing to look at what happened. I remember being mad at her when she told me that I tried to deny what was really happening. Denial didn't work.

I met with her for months. I didn't make the progress I was hoping for. She was a fine counselor who knew the Lord, but I wasn't ready to let the darkness inside me go. I lived in fear and unbelief that freedom could really exist for me. She worked well with what I told her. I was tight-lipped on the life inside my head and the horror I was beginning to remember. I didn't know what would happen if she knew it all. I wondered if I needed to move and get out of the state where much of my trauma took place before I could feel safe enough to let it all go. I discussed this with my counselor. She looked at me and said I would need to do whatever it took for healing if freedom is what I really wanted. She told me it would involve very difficult decisions at times, but it would be worth it. She encouraged me as I began to process moving out of state and what a new life might look like. I wondered if freedom might be on the other side of some difficult decisions to separate from all the darkness I knew. I had yet to find out but was willing to begin to take the risks.

Also, the Lord provided several great friends when I had difficulty and needed to get away from the horror that was taking place. However, they had difficulty with wondering what to do when my trauma began to surface. They hadn't known someone with my background before. They didn't give up on being my friend; they just explained to me that they wanted to know if they were doing the right things when something related to SRA came up. Later, a few friends made a greater investment in my healing by researching churches and many spiritual warfare avenues in the body of Christ to help me.

Though there wasn't much available that addressed DID/SRA, they started to pray for the Lord to show and provide the way for my total healing. Show and provide He did. It didn't happen overnight, but throughout the next several years, He placed person after person in my life who would provide another step in the healing process, ultimately leading me to a church that specifically ministers to those with DID/SRA.

One friend who went to my church wrote later,

> The more I got to be with her, the more questions I had and I wondered who I could talk to about what I was experiencing when we got together ... I was torn because I didn't want to sever the trust we shared. At the same time, I wondered if I was equipped to deal with what I noticed in her life as we spent more time together.
>
> I didn't feel the church would understand if I told them I had a friend who had voices inside her who wanted to talk to me. I knew my church had a strong prayer and deliverance

ministry, but I didn't feel voices inside someone would be received by the prayer team as an issue other than spiritual warfare and pertaining to the demonic world. I knew she wrestled with demonic forces, but I also knew the voices inside were different than the demonic forces she struggled with. I knew I needed to find support in being her friend. I began to pray that she would have additional people in her life who could really help her because I could only be a friend. I began to pray for support for me. I knew I couldn't keep my questions, fears, and concerns to myself or I would also be vulnerable to the darkness she struggled with. It was amazing to watch the Lord provide all the people necessary for her total healing and freedom.

Tomorrow is the meeting with Kate, Sasha, and Ken. Ken is the one they keep telling me about who works with messed-up people like me in the spiritual warfare realm. Maybe tomorrow I will finally have some relief from the torment inside. I'm thinking maybe I don't want to continue my meds, especially if they are only going to be increased every time I see my doctor. She seems to raise it for no reason. I don't need a difference. I need healing! Can't anything or anyone heal me? I don't even know anymore if it is just depression that I am always dealing with.

I should have never told anyone, especially my doctor, about when I wanted to kill myself. I think they are just after my money. Why would they care about anything else? So much for thinking I had a great doctor who understood me. But, it shouldn't take a year for my head to adjust chemically, if chemical imbalances are the problem. Is it worth taking medication when I see no difference?

My doctor was very good, though I didn't always walk out of her office thinking so. She took every issue I was having into consideration, not merely physical issues. She examined me each time, understanding I was in poor health, and aggressively tried to treat each issue. I was noncompliant to her suggestions on how to change my physical regimens. I ate poorly, because I didn't believe I deserved to be healthy. I wanted to lose excessive amounts of weight. I didn't believe life was worth living. I thought losing weight and starving myself was a slow suicide no one would catch on to. I was wrong. She had me come in with a food journal to track what my food intake was when I was consistently losing weight. I knew I ate unhealthily. I didn't want to change my eating habits. I still believed lies about myself and my value. I thought I was worthless for living and was only valuable to the kingdom of darkness and the control they had over me.

She was also very aware of the spiritual warfare and darkness active in my life. On numerous occasions she asked about recent gashes and cuts from self-mutilation like any good doctor would. I couldn't tell her. My gut told me she knew. I was afraid of her knowing. What would she think of me if she knew my life in the nights?

She was an intercessor. I knew from the way she looked. Her face had a light about her only coming from those who hide away with Him in the secret place of prayer and intercession. I had noticed this light in a few other faces, but I have found it rare. I knew she spent time with the Lord and sought His help for healing for her patients. The only reason I kept going back to her was because I knew she was praying for me.

On several occasions she asked about my severe depression and consistent thoughts of suicide. While she encouraged me to take various medications to take the edge off of the severity of my suicidal thinking, she also encouraged me to open up to my Christian counselor and others on the team who were praying for and mentoring me. Looking back, I believe she knew that much of what I was dealing with was spiritually related. I can't say this is always the case, but for me, medications weren't the answer for my depression. My depression was based on my trauma and still needing emotional and spiritual healing from the Great Physician. Other people may find medications for depression to be helpful in addition to spiritual and emotional healing. Ask the Lord what your needs are and how He wants to heal you. He ministers and heals us specific to who we are. He knows exactly what we need. He created us.

Another person on the team discipled me once a week. Every Monday after my evening class at the university, we would meet at a local coffee bookstore and read Scripture together. I had not read the gospels myself and hadn't had much experience in understanding how to read the Bible as a way to know God. I didn't want to be afraid of Scripture anymore because of the lies I believed about the Bible and the distortions I had learned. I also felt overwhelmed with thoughts of suicide and wanting to give up when I tried reading any passage of Scripture myself. Thoughts of despair and not wanting to go on surfaced when I opened the Bible. I suffered torment when I read Scripture. I know the enemy had his fingerprints in my thoughts. The strongholds of fear, unbelief, and others played their roles. Confusion and tormenting spirits would invade my understanding as I read by myself, so meeting with someone to sort this out helped tremendously.

During these times I was also able to immediately ask clarifying questions about what we were reading. This was so helpful because it quickly diffused the enemy's attempts to distort what I was reading. When I didn't understand something I could just ask about it right there, instead of letting the enemy take advantage of my misunderstanding, allowing him to plug lies in my mind during those times. Many of his schemes in how he tried to distort the Scriptures in my mind were revealed during the times my mentor and I read together. It was during this time I realized the attempts of the enemy to keep me from embracing the holy symbols of the Lord's Church because of the powerful significances of them defeating the enemy, Satan. A passion to know what the truth was and to expose everything that had been distorted in my life began to rise during this time. I began to no longer be afraid of church and all the typical triggers of church I was experiencing, but realized those very triggers were exactly what the enemy wanted me to stay away from to know all the fullness of freedom the Lord had for me. Triggers and symbols of communion, the cross, baptism, altars, and so forth, were all used in satanic ceremonies to mock the Lord and perverted to be used in horrific ways as part of my abuse. Little did I know then embracing the significance of these very symbols and items in the church would literally be the crux of my crossing over from the enemy's snare to finding total freedom. The more we read Scripture together, the more I wanted to embrace all of Christ and get rid of the darkness inside of me. The more the Lord's light of revelation from Scripture came in, the more the darkness desired was disrupted inside.

First we read the Gospel of John. Sometimes we would read other passages of Scripture, depending on how we believed the Lord was leading us in what we were learning about Him. I always treasured our times searching the Scriptures together. I always felt like I knew Him so much more after we were through reading and talking about what Scripture meant. My beliefs about Scripture changed my thinking about Him. I began to memorize specific passages I found helpful as I struggled with various tormenting thoughts throughout the day. Scriptures about overcoming fear and who God is began to renew my mind little by little. I later developed a list of scriptures to memorize for the nights, which seemed to be the worst. Before I knew it, I had an arsenal against the enemy I could use when I noticed his trying to torment me. I was no longer passive, but now, through Christ, had something to fight my enemies with. I discovered I had a will I could use; it was not dormant. My mind was active, and I realized I could make choices and decisions I felt I was never allowed to make before. This was a turning point in my healing.

What does progress in healing look like? Many view healing from DID as total integration. What if you as a helper never see complete integration occur while you are helping someone with DID? As one with DID, what if your journey of healing has taken years and the thought of integration is the furthest thing you imagine experiencing? For those with DID, it is significant that you are reading this and pursuing healing. You have made it thus far. Your pursuits for freedom and believing that healing is possible do not go unnoticed by the Deliverer and Healer.

A common lie for those with DID is they are not meeting their own or other people's expectations of where they "should be" in their healing versus where they are now. They may believe they are not making any progress. Also, this lie seems to be enforced when thoughts such as, *Look at you. People just think you are crazy! You can't call someone for the twentieth time about suicidal thoughts. They won't listen to you. They will just think that you are losing your mind if you are thinking about it so much. They will just commit you to a hospital, and what kind of progress would that be? That would just mean that you are not well and there's nothing that will really help. There will never be any hope for you if this happens so often. There must not be any way out if it has always been like this madness.*

Though I have mentioned that these thoughts and beliefs are lies, it is important to reaffirm that these thoughts indeed are lies from the pit of the enemy himself! However, wouldn't it be easy for those hurting who had thoughts like these to believe that they were not being healed or experiencing any progress in spite of any other help received? Meeting with someone, having people to call during crisis times, recognizing lies they're believing, getting up in the morning, and so on, reflects the tenacity the Lord gives them to keep on going. These actions are places of progress in the journey. As a helper, it is important to affirm when any kind of progress has taken place with the hurting person. It is likely to have taken place in many forms right before her eyes. She just may need another perspective from the Lord Himself that you can help facilitate to help her see how far she has come.

So often when hurting people don't see their progress it is easy to become hopeless and depressed. How will understanding progress help you minister to those who are hurting? Learning to recognize progress can be encouraging for one who has DID who has lost hope in this difficult journey. Keep reading. I am so glad you have persevered thus far. You must be so determined in finding healing. There is hope and healing for you.

Questions to Consider

1. Who are safe people in your life?

2. As a helper, how is the Lord leading you to be a safe person in a hurting person's life?

3. As one who is hurting, begin to ask the Lord to show you how He is safe.

4. As one who is hurting, begin to ask the Lord to bring safe people in your life who know Him closely and desire to walk with you in healing.

5. According to Isaiah 51:11, there is hope for us to enter Zion with singing. The Lord promises everlasting joy to be on our heads in freedom and wholeness. All sorrow and sighing in our lives will flee away. What do you imagine your life will look like when this becomes reality in your life? Have you ever imagined the Lord giving you such joy?

6. Ask Him to remove any doubt or unbelief you may have concerning these truths and to remove any blinders the enemy has placed over the eyes of your heart, keeping you from stepping into all truth, joy, and freedom the Lord has for you.

7. Psalm 118:6 declares that the Lord is *for* us! How does this promise resonate with you? Ask the Lord to show you His heart over you concerning this truth.

Chapter 14

What Helps Healing Along?
Setting My Face like Flint

IF I AM not spiritually aggressive, my mind does not naturally focus on the truth of what God has spoken to me in His Word. As with our physical bodies, the more tired we are, the more effort and energy we need to focus on what is reality versus how things may seem. When we are tired physically, our bodies are naturally more vulnerable to sickness. The same is true in our spiritual lives. When we are more tired spiritually, it takes more effort, requiring a conscious act of our wills to choose to believe truth instead of believing everything we think.

We must exercise our wills during this vulnerable time, or we will fall into the vulnerability of being spiritually sick. Unless we are spiritually aggressive and choose to actively believe and walk in the truth, our weariness can become fertile soil for being deceived and taken advantage of by the enemy. Begin to pray truth of what God has spoken. Even when we feel like everything inside screams against truth we are declaring, allow truth to rise up and take captive the lies opposing truth. The Word of the living God is more powerful than our own thoughts and emotions. When we choose truth, it cuts through bait tempting us to be victims to our feelings and thoughts not based on the truth of Jesus Christ.

The enemy can't read someone's thoughts. He can only put thoughts into a person's mind to make them believe those thoughts are true and to activate those thoughts with a decision based in deception. However, as long as I believe the enemy can read my thoughts and knows what I am thinking, it is easier for me to make decisions based on those thoughts. I must be vigilant about my thoughts. I must take every thought captive to the obedience of Christ as described in 2 Corinthians 10:5–6.

When we come to understand truth and it begins to transform our minds, our emotions may hold lies we cling to. Emotions are an area of our soul. When we experience emotions, lies or truth can be rooted in these places where high emotional activity occurs. For example, trauma is often associated with high emotional activity in a person. As any trauma takes place, lies the enemy wants the person to believe as a result of the trauma are often rooted in these deep emotional places.

A person who later remembers this occurrence and hasn't yet dealt with it on an emotional and spiritual level but only cognitively, may still wrestle with lies because she has subjected her beliefs to what was felt and believed. It is necessary to go to the trauma of the occurrence, because this is where lies are birthed in the mind. A lie that is easy to believe with emotions described as shame, insecurity, inadequacy, stupidity, anger, fear, can result in the thought, "I will be forced to be a child of the darkness forever." It is important to discover what the person truly believes about the situation. Ask the Lord what is true.

In this example, the person may try to find healing but only address it from cognitive angles. By this I mean she may try to find healing by simply trying to change the way she thinks. While the transformation of our minds is biblical and necessary, complete healing includes addressing lies we believe so truth can completely take their place. Promises of truth trump lies. Lies say a person is intended to be in bondage forever, and there is no way out. I now know promises such as Jeremiah 29:11 are true. My mind has changed because His truth has healed emotions of feeling trapped and believing I would be in darkness forever. His truth has literally set me free!

While this would be an appropriate verse for people to meditate on, memorize, and declare inside themselves, it may seem as though no matter how many times they quote and declare this scripture over their lives, it is making no difference. Remember, the Word of God never returns void. Though it may seem that nothing is getting better for the individuals, the Word of God is still being activated in their lives because of speaking it forth. The Word of God is alive and active, powerful, and sharper than any two-edged sword, dividing the thoughts from the soul as stated in Hebrews 4:12. Though it may seem that the Word of God is making no difference, this is not true. He is always working on their behalf.

There are other issues that may attribute to some hurting people not finding the relief they expect in meditating on the truth of Scripture. Choosing to believe the Scriptures over their life and being spiritually aggressive are the keys. The enemy will always attempt to feed us the lie that anything to build our walk with Christ will not work. The enemy will lie and say that truth of Scripture will work for everyone except me. I may see others being gloriously set free as they declare Scripture, pray, and work with others in their lives, but freedom won't ever happen for me. This is a lie from the pit of hell. The enemy will do everything in his power for us to buy his lies. Once we doubt the truth of God and what He says, we open doors to lies the enemy would love for us to believe and act upon. When we operate out of lies, we will never know our destiny and victory in Christ.

Taking Thoughts Captive

You will not reign over my thoughts tonight, enemy. I will take every thought captive tonight and make it obedient to my Lord Jesus Christ. Holy Father, I declare healing and health and wholeness over my mind. Reveal Your love to me and the alters inside. I announce a shield over my mind, where only the truth of the living God will replay and rewind itself over and over again.

God rescues us by revealing truth to us. We are responsible to replace lies with truth. God gives us the strength needed in our soul to do so. I consistently battled lies versus truth. Some lies were strangely comforting. The more I chose truth, the more whole I became. I began to choose more consistently to believe truth. I had to. There's no other way to freedom other than truth.

I am fighting. My sword feels awkward in newborn hands, but a whack here and there may make up for years lost when those enemies tried to destroy me, those unrelenting enemies of my soul.

Lie: I will never be victorious in Christ. Suicide spirits only tease; I may think for a moment that they are gone for good, but they will have their victory on dates proposed. I need to get rid of all of this emotion by throwing up. I will always be stuck having to be responsible for things I should not be responsible for. Everyone would simply move on. No one will care.

Truth: "The cords of death encompassed me, and the torrents of ungodliness terrified me. The cords of Sheol surrounded me; the snares of death confronted me. In my distress I called upon the LORD, and cried to my God for help; He heard my voice out of His temple, and my cry for help before Him came into His ears" (Ps.18:4–6). "O LORD my God, I cried to You for help, and You healed me. O LORD, You have brought up my soul from Sheol; You have kept me alive, that I would not go down to the pit" (Ps. 30:2–3).

Lie: I will never be free from others' curses over my life.

Truth: "It was for freedom that Christ set us free; therefore keep standing firm and do not be subject again to a yoke of slavery" (Gal. 5:1).

Until I learned the significance of how important it was to pay attention to what I thought and meditated on, I had no idea how much the enemy was attempting to destroy me even in my "own" thoughts. Of course, destruction has always been a scheme of his because he comes to us as the thief, killer, and destroyer (John 10:10). I did not know how much the enemy had a grip on and what he had deceived me into thinking was true.

Lord, You are revealing to me the inseparable link between the authority and power that are ours simply because we are Your children. Teach me, Father, exactly what this means. What was Your power and authority used for?

He continues to transform my mind through His Word. He alone has the words of life. He is doing a great work in my mind. Freedom is taking place. Last night I had victory. He revealed His illuminating truth in those very moments, because His liberating Scripture had penetrated within my mind and the truth was able to come forth in moments of potential disaster.

Help me, Holy Spirit, to be sensitive to what You ask. Help me realize that You have already given me the strength needed to obey what You ask. God, You have been speaking with me about my thought life and my tongue—the words I speak to myself and to others.

Importance of Affirmation of Choice

I refuse to let the enemy run uncontrollably in my thought life today. Early morning mishaps and plans set aside are no reason for my mind to be ground for the lies of the enemy. I choose right now to stop, before I go on with the rest of the morning. I want to purposefully think on His truth. I want to fill my mind with His Word, so I can combat the enemy's attacks.

Today, rather than speaking lies, I will try to only speak truth. Lies have already been exposed for my soul to see. Praise God! I recognize this pattern of lies. I recognize thoughts I am having as lies from the enemy. I choose to think about how Your love for me never ever changes. You will never ever leave me. You will always be with me while the sun rises and sets. Whether the sun is visible to me or not, You are with me. Your truth penetrates the darkness of despair. I will think about things that are lovely and worthy of praise. Thank You, Father, for enabling me to have victory through the work You have done for me.

I choose to believe Your truth. You have given me a measure of faith. I pray I am appropriately acting on this measure of faith because I am now accountable for it. I am responsible now to believe and act on Your truth. Not because my mind and my heart feel it is true, but because You have spoken truth. It doesn't matter whether or not I feel like it is true, but because it is truth, I choose to believe it. Even if I don't feel this right now, I choose to believe it anyway. Everything else is too crazy. I choose to bank on truth. I choose to declare my God is for me. My God loves me more than I will ever be able to comprehend. I choose to believe God will provide for all my needs. The truth is, He promises to order my steps and make my way perfect. With my God I shall leap over a wall and advance against a troop. I will forever be victorious with my God as my sword, shield, and buckler.

In each Scripture that the hurting person finds healing and hope, the decisions she makes to believe Scripture causes those truths to be branded in her heart. As she chooses with her will to embrace the truth—even though she may not feel like it is truth for her—lies embedded in her heart will begin to surface as truth replaces them.

One may wonder how to "choose to believe" or how to "activate my will to agree with the truth." Let's take a look at Psalm 18:33–39:

He makes my feet like hinds' feet, and sets me upon my high places. He trains my hands for battle, so that my arms can bend a bow of bronze. You have also given me the shield of Your salvation, and Your right hand upholds me; and Your gentleness makes me great. You enlarge my steps under me, and my feet have not slipped. I pursued my enemies and overtook them, and I did not turn back until they were consumed. I shattered them, so that they were not able to rise; they fell under my feet. For You have girded me with strength for battle; You have subdued under me those who rose up against me.

With these verses, one can pray and declare today, "My God will arm me and provide me with the strength I need. I choose to believe I will have the strength I need to get through today. I choose to believe that at no time today will You lead me to walk in anything except Your purposes for me. I choose to believe my feet will not stumble or flounder. Your Word says You make my feet like those of a deer. I choose to believe You will enable me to stand on these heights, even in this scary place."

One can just take the Scripture itself and make it into a prayer and an affirmation of choice. Choosing to believe what He has already promised us enables the Holy Spirit to uproot the lies. Making affirmations of truth such as this can help accelerate the process of His truth replacing the lie.

Let's try another one using Psalm 119:30–32.

I have chosen the faithful way; I have placed Your ordinances before me. I cling to Your testimonies; O LORD, do not put me to shame! I shall run the way of Your commandments, for You will enlarge my heart.

With these verses one can choose truth the Lord is showing one, especially if the person is having difficulty believing truth in memories she has. Often in memories it is common to respond in denial. The Lord wants to set us free with the truth and remove all the pain.

I choose to set my heart on Your laws. I choose to hold fast and not let go of Your statutes. I choose to believe You will not let me be put to shame. I choose to run in the paths of Your commands. I choose to believe You have set my heart free and You will continue to do so.

> The righteous cry, and the LORD hears and delivers them out of all their troubles. The LORD is near to the brokenhearted and saves those who are crushed in spirit. Many are the afflictions of the righteous; but the LORD delivers him out of them all. He keeps all his bones, not one of them is broken. Evil shall slay the wicked, and those who hate the righteous will be condemned. The LORD redeems the soul of His servants; and none of those who take refuge in Him will be condemned.
>
> —Psalm 34:17–22

> Therefore, do not throw away your confidence, which has a great reward. For you have need of endurance, so that when you have done the will of God, you may receive what was promised. For yet in a very little while, He who is coming will come, and will not delay. But My righteous one shall live by faith; and if he shrinks back, My soul has no pleasure in him. But we are not of those who shrink back to destruction, but of those who have faith to the preserving of the soul.
>
> —Hebrews 10:35–39

Jesus, I thank You for changing my life this week. Your Holy Spirit has moved in my life. You invite me to search Your words. I'm learning to dig for treasures of Your truth. I'm learning it is my responsibility to search the Scriptures myself and discover truth for myself. I want to soak it in, meditate on it, and allow it to renew my mind. Lord, change the very essence of how I think. I want to know Your Word like never before. I hunger to know Your truth and allow it to change who I am. Please, God, teach me Your ways.

Dismantling Strongholds

I will use the stronghold of fear as an example of one spirit to dismantle. You can use the principles based on Scripture to begin to dismantle any stronghold in your life. Choose to separate the lies you believe with truth as the Lord shows you in His Word. Many thoughts related to fear are based on lies.

God, show me any fear my heart has fallen prey to. Show me what Your truth is concerning this.

Lie: If I still feel afraid after asking God for peace, there must be something wrong with me. I must not have enough faith if I still struggle with fear.

Truth: The enemy wants me to believe this struggle is only about me, and that I am a failure. Satan doesn't want me to think any of this has to do with him. I can forbid the enemy from bothering me in any way today (James 4:8; Eph. 6:10-12; John 10:10).

> The thief comes only to steal and kill and destroy; I came that they may have life and have it abundantly.
> —John 10:10

> Draw near to God and He will draw near to you. Cleanse your hands, you sinners; and purify your hearts, you double-minded.
> —James 4:8

> Finally, be strong in the Lord and in the strength of His might. Put on the full armor of God, so that you will be able to stand firm against the schemes of the devil. For our struggle is not against flesh and blood, but against the rulers, against

the powers, against the world forces of this darkness, against
the spiritual forces of wickedness in the heavenly places.
—Ephesians 6:10–12

Lie: If anyone knew what fears I dealt with, they would think
I was crazy. They wouldn't believe I was a Christian.

Truth: "Therefore, confess your sins to one another, and
pray for one another so that you may be healed. The effective
prayer of a righteous man can accomplish much" (James 5:16).

Dwelling on thoughts of fear is sin. When I don't choose to
believe the truth God has already promised me, I am choosing to
believe lies of the enemy. Believing the enemy's lies over God's
truth is sin. Pump in truth to get lies exposed. Lies oppose the
truth. If the truth is pumped in, there may be opposition inside
as the truth is received or not received.

One of the keys to move healing along is perseverance and
determination that only comes from the Lord. In our weariness,
it is normal to become so tired to the point of losing hope and
wondering if we will ever be any better or if things will be any
different. Allow me to encourage you as one who has walked
this road that, yes, it does get better, and freedom does come.

A good way I knew whether or not I believed a lie was to
quote truth relating to what I thought about. If an alter was
really resisting the truth, oftentimes a lie was being believed by
an alter needing to be addressed. Once I came to understand
I believed a lie, the Lord showed me that I don't have to keep
beliefs I don't want. It was merely a matter of choice for me
when I discovered I could believe the truth. I declared with my
mouth what was true and renounced the lie I had believed.

I declared that I had a sound mind and I didn't need to
fear the confusion taking place. I declared God was holding
me up. With my mouth I resisted the enemy's attempts to
discourage me and cause me to think there was no hope for me
or my mind with all its confusion. I declared God's plans for

me will continue to be plans of hope and a future that involved a completely sound mind. I continued to resist the enemy and draw closer to the Lord and His truth. The lies began to fade. The enemy had to flee. He can't stand hearing the Word of the Lord, especially spoken out of the same mouth of the person he is attempting to destroy.

Shut Doors Where My Enemy Had Access

I will first share what I learned concerning how to be spiritually aggressive as I read the Scriptures more regularly.

These days it has been easier to read the Bible because I don't get headaches and dizziness. The words on the Bible's pages don't scramble as often.

I have more insight as I read the Old Testament concerning how serious the Lord was when He required that the Israelites remove idols and the things they worshipped that were not glorifying to the Lord Himself. He didn't want those people to worship those things or those idols because it led them to believe lies, and that led to destruction of their lives

The Lord's truth and declarations over me stand victorious whether or not I am emotionally strong. The Lord Himself has declared I will not fold in and collapse within these lies. He stated that He will rescue my mind from all the fiery darts of the enemy.

Ways the Enemy Desires to Deceive Believers
(teaching from Lydia Discipleship Ministries)

1. Overriding the prompting of the Holy Spirit to be cautious

2. Entertaining prideful thoughts

3. Talking to evil spirits to gain information about what to do next

4. Practicing the idolatry of relying on a specific method instead of relying on the Holy Spirit and His leading

5. Responding only on the basis of need and not on discernment

6. Not asking the Lord about leadings, impressions, feelings, or seemingly non-sensical promptings

7. Craving the adrenalin rush of hand-to-hand combat with the forces of darkness

8. Having an incorrect/unbalanced view of spiritual warfare

> Jesus said to them, "If God were your Father, you would love Me, for I proceeded forth and have come from God, for I have not even come on My own initiative, but He sent Me. Why do you not understand what I am saying? It is because you cannot hear My word. You are of your father the devil, and you want to do the desires of your father. He was a murderer from the beginning, and does not stand in the truth, because there is no truth in him. Whenever he speaks a lie, he speaks from his own nature; for he is a liar and the father of lies."
>
> —John 8:42–44

> "And you will know the truth, and the truth will make you free." They answered Him, "We are Abraham's descendent, and have never yet been enslaved to anyone; how is it that You say, 'You will become free'?" Jesus answered them, "Truly, truly, I say to you, everyone who commits sin is the slave of sin. The slave does not remain in the house forever; the son does remain forever. So if the Son makes you free, you will be free indeed."
>
> —John 8:32–36

God knows that the battle for whether or not we live our lives based on truth or on lies is in our minds. He knows this decision is our choice to make. It is our choice to live either by our feelings and lies or to take thoughts captive, making them obedient to Christ. This will determine victory over lies as believers in Jesus Christ. The enemy also knows our mind is the battleground. One of easiest ways the enemy tries to destroy our lives is by convincing us to believe every thought we have, even those planted by him. This causes us to be a slave to our flesh, the world, and the enemy himself.

Questions to Consider

1. Ask the Lord how He desires truth to transform you. What is the significance of steeping your mind in truth?

2. What is the difference between knowing truth and believing truth? What causes your heart to cross over to believing truth?

3. Why is it important to use your will and choose to believe truth even when you don't feel like doing so?

4. What does it mean to take thoughts captive? What does this look like on a moment-by-moment basis?

5. Ask the Lord if there are any open doors you have left for the enemy to gain access to your heart and mind. Repent and shut them as the Lord speaks to you specifically about those areas.

6. What does it mean to be spiritually aggressive? Ask the Lord what truths He wants to reveal to you concerning your authority and stance of victory in Him.

7. Ask the Lord if there is any deception known or unknown operating in your life and what truths He wants to replace it with.

Chapter 15

Spiritual Warfare: Having a Biblical and Balanced Perspective

⚬⚬⚬

THIS TIME AS I write, I am a different person than the one who wrote of coffins and ropes of death. Jesus came and delivered me from all that bound me. I chose to forgive. I repented of my sin, all of it. I repented of my past generations' sin. I renounced the lies I have believed and replaced them with the truth.

Jesus has rescued me from death; He is restoring my aching soul. I can stand firmly and say that Jesus really loves me. Thank You for removing the spirit of death, the mocker, shame, guilt, the silencer, confusion, anger, bitterness, and self-hatred. How can I ever thank You for removing these bondages out of my life? I have never felt so free, amazing, whole, and clean. I feel as though the grave clothes and ropes have literally been peeled and shaken off of me, and I have been clothed with His new garments of praise. He clothed me with a bleach-white dress, more beautiful than I could have dreamed. Jesus, You are truly the Healer and the Deliverer of my soul. It is true; if the Son sets you free you are free indeed. I will never in my life forget the afternoon of the conference.

Hindering spirits ensnaring me are gone. I shut many doors, and the darkness bothering me has been forced to leave because of my prayers and asking Him to heal me.

Lies have no authority in my life any longer. I want to stand on His truth. I want truth to reign. I want it to change who I am. I want truth to change my identity. The past is now behind me. I press on to what He has for me. There's no condemnation on me because I am in Jesus. There's no shame in me. Peace like I have never known before resides inside. I am no longer afraid of His holy and loving presence. Guilt and fear no longer control me. Instead, acceptance, love, and forgiveness radiate inside like the sun has risen and taken away all the darkness of nights I knew. Life is different inside of me.

I believe He loves me; He really loves me. Jesus loves me. Not only do I know it cognitively, but I now believe this truth in the deepest places of my heart I never thought His truths would go. I want His truth to continually transform every area of my life. He really does love me. Jesus loves me and desires the best for me. He treasures and cherishes me. He rejoices over me with singing even tonight. I see Him smiling over me, so proud to call me His beloved daughter. He loves me with His everlasting love.

While this is a representation of real experiences and encounters with Jesus Christ, He really began to change me inside. I did not realize it at the time, but He was not done healing me. At this point I thought since Jesus met me and did so much then, I should be fine now and would not struggle any more with the same issues that I had always faced. This was not the case. Jesus did a great work in me on numerous occasions. But because that was the beginning of a process that was in His perfect timing, walking out my healing and freedom was yet to come. Being delivered from what He set me free from did not mean that I would never have to deal with those same spirits again or that there weren't any others to deal with that had a grip in my life. It did mean that I was on the road of healing and that He would walk with me every step of the way. He would not rush me into what I couldn't handle. He would not leave me alone to deal with the aftermath of His changes inside of me. This was when alters were most stirred up as their territory and how things were inside were drastically beginning to change.

My perspective on spiritual warfare was that once deliverance happened, healing would happen automatically. Many times of deliverance occurred in my life. Was I a failure because I needed multiple sessions of being delivered from the darkness inside? No. Each time, He had His purposes in mind that were ordained by Him to bring full healing. Each time led to the next step of freedom needed. Each time I chose to open my heart more to what He desired to heal. Each time I came to a place of new trust to allow Him into where I was broken.

I discovered Jesus was using deliverance as part of my healing, but He didn't heal me with just one session of deliverance. The enemy wanted me to be discouraged when I wasn't totally free each time I met for a session of prayer/healing ministry. I did not understand why I continued to feel defeated. After all, I had been "set free." Why was I struggling so much still? I did not have a biblical, appropriate perspective of spiritual warfare and how God wanted me whole more than I did. Graciously, He began to teach me. I continued to be healed and set free as He walked me out of the chains that bound me for so long.

The enemies against my soul couldn't get through the helmet of salvation the Lord has given me. Darkness was shooting arrows and curses as they marched around us. They made their curses attempting to penetrate the invisible hedge of protection, the firewall that the Lord created about me. Darkness kept hitting the firewall surrounding me. They could not get through to harm me. They became more frustrated the longer and harder they tried. The hedge would not allow them to touch me or hurt me in any way.

I learned through these occasions that the enemy is the most patient created being. He will wait if necessary for me to open the door to him on any occasion to get access to my heart and mind to attempt again to destroy and kill me. He is always on the lookout for opportunities to cause my complete demise. Should I be afraid of him because of his aggressive and sneaky attempts to kill me or keep me in bondage forever? Absolutely not. I was still learning this truth.

I must be losing my mind if lamps randomly fall off my desk for no reason. What is going on? What spirits dwell inside of me? How can they get out completely forever? When will they no longer be inside of me? When will they realize that I no longer want them inside of me? When will they cease to threaten? What do I need to do to make them go away? What is with this programming? Is that applicable to me? How would I know? Am I just completely making all of this more complicated than it really is? Jesus, You are the One who can bring me freedom. Show me the way of truth.

A biblically based and balanced perspective on spiritual warfare includes several truths that become keys to freedom. Truth and spiritual warfare within the discipling/counseling context involves teaching the person to stand in the reality of her identity in Christ by understanding truth in how to take authority in Christ to resist the enemy and see him run from her life. The core of training someone in spiritual warfare is encouraging her to know and walk in truth. The Bible is clear concerning freedom and how truth is inextricably linked to being free: "You shall know the truth and the truth shall make you free" (John 8:32).

It is sometimes necessary for the person to close specific doors that have been opened by her or for her (as in generational issues) and evict the demonic forces that are within her. This is done through prayer. There are subtle differences between a typical "deliverance ministry" and being involved in spiritual warfare with a hurting person/counselee. A deliverance ministry may deal with spirits that are oppressing someone and exorcise them from the person over one or several times, depending on the severity of the influence the spirits have had on the person. Depending on different ancestral or generational sins or curses, it may be more than one event to ensure that such spirits and sins are dealt with thoroughly. Going through deliverance sessions can be very beneficial for some hurting people.

In the discipleship/counseling context role of working with hurting people, spiritual warfare may not necessarily involve evicting demons and deliverance in that particular way but will be an area for the hurting person to discover the spiritual world and how to walk in authority as she learns who she is in Christ. This is not to exclude the method of evicting demons that may obviously have a grip in the hurting person's life, because that may be needed. However, as we disciple and counsel we must keep in mind that deliverance is not all that is needed for the person to be completely victorious in her Christian life. Allow me to explain.

A goal in understanding balanced, biblical spiritual warfare is to recognize deception. When we are deceived, a door is opened for the enemy to continue to lie to us. As we continue to ask the Lord to show us any areas we may be deceived, He will show us the truth about the reality of spiritual warfare and why we must understand our role in the war He has placed us in to win! When we understand we are victors in Christ and learn our identity in Him, the truth of who God is, and the truth about our enemy, Satan, we can stand victoriously over all powers of darkness that would attempt to oppose us. When we understand that spiritual warfare is not a power encounter against the enemy and our Lord Jesus Christ, or a teeter-totter battle that constantly rages, we begin to see the authority we have in Christ. Spiritual warfare is a battle of truth versus lies, and a war of who we allow to have authority in our thought lives. The enemy would love for us to believe that our war is a power encounter with him. As long as we believe that lie, we have lost ground in our victory in Christ. However, when the

Lord reveals the authority we have in Christ and that the battle is already won because of His death and resurrection from the grave, we begin to walk as those who have authority over the enemy and have victory over darkness.

Several keys the Lord had been imparting were aspects of spiritual warfare and how to understand my enemy. More importantly, the Lord taught me who I am in Him. Believing who I am in Christ made the difference in how I learned to operate in my authority in Christ while working with alters inside of me. The following is reference from teachings from Deeper Walk International and Mark Bubeck, author of *The Adversary*.

When it comes to spiritual warfare, we basically have three enemies. These three enemies include the world, our flesh, and the devil. In order to believe in spiritual warfare we must believe in the reality of Satan and what he tries to accomplish in a believer's life. We must acknowledge there is a global battle between Satan and Jesus Christ.

> Therefore, since the children share in flesh and blood, He Himself likewise also partook of the same, that through death He might render powerless him who had the power of death, that is, the devil.
>
> —Hebrews 2:14

> Again there was a day when the sons of God came to present themselves before the LORD, and Satan also came among them to present himself before the LORD. . . . The LORD said to Satan, "Have you considered My servant Job? For there is no one like him on the earth, a blameless and upright man fearing God and turning away from evil. And he still holds fast his integrity, although you incited Me against him to ruin him without cause."
>
> —Job 2:1, 3

You know of Jesus of Nazareth, how God anointed Him with the Holy Spirit and with power, and how He went about doing good and healing all who were oppressed by the devil, for God was with Him.

—Acts 10:38

And he laid hold of the dragon, the serpent of old, who is the devil and Satan, and bound him for a thousand years.

—Revelation 20:2

We must acknowledge the existence of evil spirits.

And the great dragon was thrown down, the serpent of old who is called the devil and Satan, who deceives the whole world; he was thrown down to the earth, and his angels were thrown down with him.

—Revelation 12:9

We must believe Satan can oppress Christians.

And at the same time they also learn to be idle, as they go around from house to house; and not merely idle, but also gossips and busybodies, talking about things not proper to mention. . . . give the enemy no occasion for reproach; for some have already turned aside to follow Satan.

—1 Timothy 5:13–15

What is the enemy's role in the spiritual battle we cannot see but are influenced by? What is the enemy's role in woundedness?

Satan's Role in Woundedness

1. He causes the wounding (past).
2. He tries to prevent healing (present).
3. He intensifies the pain and the extent of the woundedness (future).

Can Christians have wicked spirits? Some believe Satan or his demons cannot indwell a believer; the Holy Spirit and an evil spirit cannot inhabit the same body. This idea stems from the belief that a Christian is fully equipped to meet the fiery darts of the enemy, the armor is for external and internal foes, the believer is delivered from the power of Satan and his demons, and it was Christ's purpose to destroy the works of the devil.

Terminology needs to be clarified: possession versus "demonized" (oppressed). Does the believer have limitations on the protection God has armed her with? What if the believer doesn't resist the enemy (James 4:7)? We are made free from sin (Rom. 6:6–7), but if we don't reckon ourselves dead to sin, choose truth, or walk in the Spirit, doors to the enemy will open, giving access to his destruction in our lives (Rom. 6:11–13; Gal. 5:16). When this happens are we hopeless to the enemy's schemes of destruction? No way! All we have to do is repent, shut and remove the doors of deception we opened, choose truth, and walk in our authority in Christ. Victory is ours no matter how many times we have been deceived by the enemy. God wants us free and walking in complete victory and truth!

Armor is a protection against penetration. If the Christian does not obey the command to put on the armor, he or she is vulnerable to invasion. Specific commands regarding resisting the devil would not be needed if the enemy couldn't influence us (Eph. 4:27; 2 Cor. 2:11; 1 Peter 5:8; 2 Cor. 11:4). There is no verse that says that a Christian can't have the Holy Spirit and wicked spirits oppressing him or her. A believer will never belong to the enemy of darkness again and therefore will never be possessed by the enemy. Once we choose to follow Jesus Christ with our lives, He is the only One who possesses and keeps us. We belong to Jesus Christ, and this belonging is totally safe. We have nothing to fear when we belong to Christ.

Misconceptions about Dealing with Demonic Forces

1. Every problem a person has is caused by Satan.
2. Once you evict a demon from a person, that person is automatically, forever free in that area.
3. There is always a show of power by the demon as it is being evicted.
4. People always throw up when a demon leaves them.
5. A demon must always manifest itself (take over the person) to be cast out.
6. Only specially gifted Christians can "do deliverance."
7. One must know the name of a demon in order to evict it.
8. There is always a struggle and lots of shouting before a demon leaves.
9. You have to get information from the demon in order to understand how it has been working before it will leave.
10. It is dangerous to work against wicked spirits because they will always retaliate or enter you or someone in your family.

Basics about Our Enemy, Satan

> …so that no advantage would be taken of us by Satan, for we are not ignorant of his schemes.
> —2 Corinthians 2:11

God is greater than Satan and we, as Christians, are in Christ. We do not need to be frightened by Satan, nor should we be fascinated by his work.

Lord, should any of my views about Satan and warfare be changed? Help me understand the truth of my union with Christ and what it means in my everyday life.

Names Scripture Uses for Satan

Deceiver

> For such men are false apostles, deceitful workers, disguising
> themselves as apostles of Christ. No wonder, for even Satan
> disguises himself as an angel of light.
>
> —2 Corinthians 11:13–14

*Lord, please begin to show me how Satan has been trying to
hinder my walk with You. How has he deceived me? Are there any
experiences that I may have accepted as being from You that were
not? Thank You for giving me discernment. I pray in the name of
Jesus Christ, amen.*

Accuser

> Then I heard a loud voice in heaven, saying, "Now the
> salvation, and the power, and the kingdom of our God and
> the authority of His Christ have come, for the accuser of our
> brethren has been thrown down, he who accuses them before
> our God day and night."
>
> —Revelation 12:10

Satan accuses God, telling us lies about what He is like,
about His character. Satan also accuses us, telling us lies and
distortions about ourselves. He wants us to hate ourselves. He
also accuses other people and tries to stir up bitterness and hatred
in our hearts toward them.

*Lord Jesus, how does Satan accuse You to me? What distortions
about You have I accepted? What lies or distortions about myself
need to be uprooted from my mind and my emotions? How can they
be uprooted? Please show me, in Jesus' name.*

Liar

> . . . the devil . . . does not stand in the truth because there is no truth in him. Whenever he speaks a lie, he speaks from his own nature, for he is a liar and the father of lies.
>
> —John 8:44b

Anything that does not match up to what the Bible says is a lie. We should test what we think is true by looking to see if Scripture agrees or disagrees with it.

Lord Jesus, show me any areas where I have accepted Satan's lies. I want to have truth in my innermost being. Thank You for teaching me. Show me how to use Your Word as the Sword of the Spirit as I confront the lies with Your truth. I pray in the name of Jesus Christ, amen.

Destroyer/Murderer

> They have as king over them, the angel of the abyss; his name in Hebrew is Abaddon, and in the Greek he has the name Apollyon. [*Apollyon* means destroyer.]
>
> —Revelation 9:11

> Be of sober spirit, be on the alert. Your adversary, the devil, prowls around like a roaring lion, seeking someone to devour.
>
> —1 Peter 5:8

Satan tries to destroy our lives. He tries anything to destroy God in us.

Tempter

> And He was in the wilderness forty days being tempted by Satan; and He was with the wild beasts, and the angels were ministering to Him.
>
> —Mark 1:13

Lord Jesus, help me to choose life. Help me recognize when Satan is tempting me to choose his way.

Satan may try to do other things as well. He tries to keep us from understanding the Bible (Mark 4:15); he causes some illnesses (Luke 13:16); he tries to control us and make us his slave (2 Tim. 2:26). Always remember: Christ is Victor over Satan!

How Does a Wicked Spirit Enter/Influence a Person?

1. By invitation, known or unknown
2. By exposure to demonic spirits through the occult, movies, games, music
3. Trauma (an emotionally traumatic event is a spiritual event)
4. Sent by someone else
5. Generational occultism
6. Spiritual deception

How Does a Person Get Rid of a Wicked Spirit or Its Influence?

1. By pumping in the truth
2. If specifically invited or sent, by specifically closing the door (place of entrance) and commanding it to leave
3. By standing in her authority that is in the name of Jesus and through His blood
4. Prevent re-entry by being spiritually aggressive

How Does Satan Specifically Influence a Helper or Hurting Person?

1. Hindrances/opposition/interference
   Fog
   Accusation

Prevent from coming to an appointment where two will meet

Stirring up inappropriate fear

2. Hiding key information

Person forgets events

3. Embedding lies

Prevent them from absorbing/remembering truth

Provides a resistance to truth

4. Pressure for suicide
5. Demonic presence
6. Adding rage to anger
7. Retaliation afterward

Practical Things to Do:

1. Hang doorpost signs, Scripture verses in your office.
2. Have a Bible visible.
3. Have a prayer team/person.
4. Have someone with the gift of discerning of spirits on your team.
5. Think through what Satan is attempting to accomplish and refuse to go there.

How a Helper Could Pray for the Hurting Person:

1. Give me God's *agape* love for the hurting person.
2. Keep me from deception.
3. Give us discernment to see the real, core issues.
4. Remove any demonic resistance to the truth.
5. Help her do hard things.
6. May she have truth in her innermost being.
7. Silence the accuser of the brethren.
8. Defeat the destroyer.
9. Help her to be teachable and willing to change.
10. Remove barriers to hungering for Your Word.

11. Provide a church with discipleship training that can help them grow spiritually.
12. Help them to be bold against any internal threats of blackmail.
13. Help us understand more about our union with Christ and the work of the cross of Christ.
14. Help us understand more about our authority in Christ and how to use it against the enemy.
15. Help me to resist fear.

In the battle of spiritual warfare, the key is remembering we are victors in Christ. We have authority in Christ over all the power and lies of the enemy. As we engage in walking in who we are in Christ and in the ministry of helping others, we also need to be mindful that we are now a specific target for the enemy. The enemy hates believers walking in truth themselves, but he especially hates it when they go after others to help them find freedom in Christ. Does this mean we all need to walk in fear if we want to help someone get free? Absolutely not. Greater is the Lord who is in us than the enemy who is in the world. We have all victory in Christ. As we continue to take up the armor of God in our lives as Ephesians 6 commands us to, we will be equipped to overcome and stand in who we are and what the Lord specifically calls each of us to do.

We are all in a battle, whether we consider ourselves as part of ministry or the prayer/healing ministry. It doesn't matter if we are involved with functions of our church, if we volunteer, or do nothing at all. The enemy is after believers to destroy and kill them if they are in Christ. But it does make the enemy particularly nervous if we also decide to walk in all the areas the Lord calls us to, as that is a direct threat against the enemy's plans for other people's lives. However, remember again, we have all authority and power in Christ to trample on snakes and scorpions as the Lord calls us into particular areas of ministry.

Does this mean to minister to whomever without protection from your local church because you are completely covered in Christ? No. Scripture calls us to be sober and vigilant as the roaring lion comes to seek and destroy whomever he may devour. The enemy works overtime on those who choose to abandon themselves to Christ. For this reason, we must have all the prayer covering we can through our local church body in Christ and others. Not because we will be defeated if we do not have this covering, but without prayer covering and discernment from others who hear from the Lord, we are more vulnerable. We may set ourselves up for deception via the thoughts the enemy feeds us, and we may not know the difference when the enemy is lying to us in order to cause our ultimate destruction.

Prayer is potentially our best weapon and our best defense as we draw close to our Deliverer and bombard the gates of hell for those still in bondage. Prayer allows us to be open before the Lord for any deception that we may still believe and need to be free from. Only the Lord can deliver us from deception. Only God can teach us what truth is. When we remain in Him He exposes all truth to us, and we are continually set free to be victorious.

Questions to Consider

1. Go back through each of the prayers throughout the chapter and process with the Lord what He shows you through each of them.

2. Ask the Lord to show you how to guard against schemes of the enemy concerning spiritual warfare.

3. What fears might you have concerning spiritual warfare? Be open with the Lord about them and allow Him to show you the truth about each of them.

4. Ask the Lord for strategies for how He wants you to walk and stand in your authority in Christ and as you minister to the hurting.

5. Ask the Lord to show you any views concerning spiritual warfare that need to be changed.

6. What is the role of the enemy in woundedness?

7. What is our role in Christ as He calls us to minister to the shattered?

Chapter 16

In the Meantime of Integration

~❦~

IT IS HELPFUL to remember that it won't always be like this. I don't know why it's so painful right now. I don't know why it feels so much like I am going backward in my healing sometimes, because I feel more like I am just going crazy. Focusing on what I do know and the promises that God has already said about me is what I try to hang on to during times like these.

We don't want to meet with Kate 'cause her friend will be with her and we don't know her. She will just think that all of us are crazy. It seems as though every time we think someone will understand that we are sorry, the noise and peeps from the alters are let out.

A friend of Kate is meeting with me so she can learn about working with us. What do you mean, "working with us"? What is this about being trained just to talk to me, as though we are some sort of project for eager ears pursuing psychology doctorates or some other official credential? Why can't anyone just listen to help us? Are they just using us to make a better living? What is so complicated about that?

Why is she suddenly so curious about me? Why does she want to tell all her friends who want to help broken people about me? Does that mean I am broken? Why can't she just listen instead of so quickly wanting me to be fixed so that I am normal like everyone else? I hide behind a plastic smile.

Jesus is sovereign in how He chooses to heal any of us. In my journey, what became necessary was being part of an intensive, spiritually activated, alive church that was fully engaged to see those in bondage set free. It was at this church that the majority of my healing took place.

No matter how significant my freedom and healing may be, I know He will not ever be completely finished. I know this because He is always transforming us into the likeness of His image so that we are more and more like Him. I am learning that God is so passionate about our having a close relationship with Him that He desires us to come to know Him and His character even more than He desires to only remove pain in our lives. Why is this? Why does knowing Him and having a close intimate relationship with Him exceed removing pain? Doesn't He know how much this hurts? How does knowing Him relate to why He won't remove pain we face in our healing? Isn't this a way of God saying that our pain is not as big as we say it is? Is God in the business of minimizing our pain? Is our knowing Him all He cares about just so that He gets more attention? Does He really care all that much about what is going on inside of us?

By daily steeping my mind in truth, it was revealed why God is so passionate about our knowing Him and how pursuing a closer relationship with Him directly correlates to our continued healing and freedom. When I asked the Lord to free me in so many different areas, I was bothered by His response many times. My prayers usually were something like, "Please don't let me fall on my face and give in to the enemy's temptations tonight because I know this keeps me in this bondage. Please help me with this. Free me from this struggle."

I remember one time His response so clearly: "I wish you knew how much I love you." I blew off His response because I didn't understand it, and I thought, *What does that have to do with my being rescued from this huge temptation I have tonight?* I did not understand His response because I did not know Him the way that He wished. He is passionate about our knowing Him and His true character, a view without any distortions. We don't recognize the distortions we have of Him until He reveals His truth in His Word through His Holy Spirit.

When His response to me was later brought back to my spirit, I was surprised that it was coming back to my memory. I wondered why the words seemed so vividly clear when they didn't seem to make any sense to me when I first heard them. Those words kept ringing in my mind. I couldn't stop thinking about them. Finally, I asked the Lord, *What do You mean by "I wish you knew how much I love you"?* Later that night I was reading about God having an everlasting love for us: that He has the very hairs of our head numbered and that He knows when we rise in the morning and when we lay our heads to rest. He knows the words on our tongues before we speak them (Ps. 139). I felt like the Lord was saying, "I know you inside and out. I want you to know Me and My character just as well." Still, I thought, *What does that have to do with my pain?*

When we are confronted with truth, such as Jesus having greater love for us than anyone else is capable of, it is difficult to accept when we do not have an accurate view of God and His character. One of the reasons why God is so passionate about our knowing Him instead of just being healed by Him is so that we can correctly associate His truth with who He is and open ourselves up to Him to be that in our lives. We cannot come to a place of accurately understanding Scripture until we equally come to a place of intimately knowing Him. The more closely we know Him, the more clearly truth is revealed in our lives. When this happens, we are set free. Knowing Him has everything to do with His continued healing and freedom in our lives.

Often when I didn't understand His timing and why this whole process did not happen at a faster pace, I did not understand His grace. The Bible says that God will never give us anything that is too big for us to handle. This means that He will not bring to my dreams, or to my memory, or bring up any trigger that I will not be able to handle. God knows exactly how much we can physically, emotionally, and spiritually handle at any given time.

> But now, thus says the LORD, your Creator, O Jacob, and He who formed you, O Israel, "Do not fear, for I have redeemed you; I have called you by name; you are Mine! When you pass through the waters, I will be with you; and through the rivers, they will not overflow you. When you walk through the fire, you will not be scorched, nor will the flame burn you. For I am the LORD your God, the Holy One of Israel, your Savior. I have given Egypt as your ransom, Cush and Seba in your place."
>
> —Isaiah 43:1–3

He will not give us anything beyond what we can bear, as the healing process may take longer than we may desire or expect. I remember a friend of mine who had surgery on her foot, and she was allergic to the metal her doctor normally used for this particular surgery. The doctors did not listen to the warning of the allergy and thought it was easier and faster if they did it the way they felt. My friend had a severe infection in her foot and the inside exploded, ultimately taking the foot much longer to heal enough to have to go in for an additional surgery. When we are impatient with our own healing and think it best to rush the Lord, we may be in for a longer road than we wanted. Allow Him to move in His timing. He wants us to learn to wait and come to know Him more intimately in the meantime, absorbing more of His truth, resulting in more and more freedom.

Perseverance

So everything seems great outside of the stuff happening inside of me that continues to rage and mock truth as I continue to heal. I feel like this darkness is going to rip apart my insides and shred me physically or take control of my body when I don't want them to. I must be crazy. I really want these things to come out. I am so afraid of knowing everything that happened that I have blocked out.

It may be worth mentioning that those who live with DID have persevered and fought their whole lives to this point. They are some of the most determined people you may ever have the privilege to know. I once heard a theory that one of the enemy's schemes against believers is if he can't get a believer to fall into an obvious sin, he will try to wear out the believer, causing him to become lazy in his faith. He is drained by Christian activities and religious duties and finds himself sapped of the very life and power of God he lives to proclaim and testify of. What happens to a believer if she is just plain tired and weary of the godly tasks at hand, making her want to quit?

In the life of a hurting person it seems as though this scheme is even more pronounced with the enemy's lies echoing in her weariness, wondering if life will ever be better, any less painful, or any less crazy. Sometimes it is difficult for Christians who don't deal with DID to recall the times that the Lord has moved and acted on their behalf when they were struggling with not much light at the end of the tunnel. In the psalms, David talks about the times that the Lord remembered him and answered his cries. David told his own soul to be encouraged in the Lord: "Soul, why so downcast? Put your hope in God." What does this mean to the hurting person who has not known how to hope?

In this process of learning how to persevere I will mention a few things I personally found extremely helpful: writing in my journal and recounting the Lord's faithfulness on a daily basis; talking to a helper daily to discuss what went right versus what went wrong and was crazy; reminding myself of the promises that I was focusing on that particular day; and giving myself time off to rest, play, and rejuvenate from chaos that lived inside of me.

What might be significant to write about when you are thinking about giving up? What does it mean to recount the faithfulness of the Lord? Go through your day from the time you got up to the point you are at now and write everything you did that day—everything you were involved with, good and bad; the people you saw; the places you went; describe the room; anything that may come to your mind.

You could write how the Lord was faithful in keeping you alive through the night before. He kept you safe in nightmares you may have had. Even here you are recounting the Lord's faithfulness and goodness, just because you woke up.

If you got out of bed and were able to get dressed in a reasonable time you can recount the faithfulness of the Lord by enabling you to make choices that were safe. You were able to activate your will and weren't forced to wear something you didn't want to wear. He now has you in a place where you can choose different things that help you throughout your day. You are no longer trapped in a place where you couldn't do this.

Continue throughout the rest of the day taking the things that happened, as small or large as they may seem to you. Write how He is faithful to you. Especially during this time when you wonder if this will ever pass, it is most important to choose to believe that He has a hope and good plans for you. Don't let the enemy win, because he will try to make you think that you will never get better. Remember, it won't always be like this.

Absorbing Truth in Bite-Sized Pieces

Sometimes the thought of reading or memorizing Scripture, as encouraged in most churches, can be really overwhelming for one who is hurting. It may be overwhelming because of the spiritual opposition she often faces as she attempts to get close to any truth of Scripture. Dealing with so much emotionally and spiritually, it may be difficult for her to grasp anything specific out of numerous books and chapters. It's like trying to find the needle for taking the splinter out of her life in a haystack of verses.

During times of so much opposition and difficulty, I found that reading one verse would help me. I often found the psalms to be appropriate places for my soul to relate to, as when David continually cried out for the Lord to rescue him from his enemies. When I found a verse I could understand, after the blurriness and fog went away (spiritual opposition) and I could see the verse for what it said, I rewrote it into one sentence that I could hang on to. For example, Psalm 144:11 (NIV) says, "Deliver me and rescue me from the hands of foreigners whose mouths are full of lies, whose right hands are deceitful." I wrote, "He will deliver and rescue me from the liars and from those who have deceived me for so long." I kept this promise in my jeans pocket and frequently pulled it out to remind myself when I was having a difficult time. At any point in the day I could be reminded of that promise. No matter how long it took to absorb this one truth, I would hang on to it until I believed it.

Later, I realized that because the enemy had had all my life to establish his lies inside of me, it would take a while for me to lay new ground of truth. In the Lord's graciousness when I still became discouraged thinking, *I am not as far along as I should be,* and heard the accuser of the brethren in my spiritual ears, the Lord continued to show me it takes time to lay a foundation of truth. Truth cannot be laid on sand, but rocks built on His truth will last an eternity. Rock by rock, promise by promise, His truths were laid. I absorbed His Word bit by bit. I was creating a new foundation in my soul.

How to Minister to Alters as the Lord Leads

Can't we sit in the back?

I don't like this place. Can we go somewhere else for the morning?

What are we wearing this for? I never wear this when I sell things at work.

The man is wearing a red rose on his suit. Can we get away from him?

I don't like it here. I am surrounded by people on every side, and I feel like I can't even breathe. It is not safe in here. Can we please leave?

The man over there keeps walking back and forth toward us. If he gets any closer I am going to get out of here.

I was visiting a new church for the third time. I kept going back because I liked the worship and thought they had good teaching. I was being fed there for the time being. I also didn't have regular transportation to church at the time, so any ride I could get to any church was what I took. Most of the people I knew went to this particular church, so I rode with them.

This particular morning, some alters inside were having a difficult time being there. Being a rather large church of several thousand, the auditorium was pretty full. People stood right next to me when we sang during the worship service. I was near an aisle where ushers walked back and forth to scope the rare empty seat that could be filled by latecomers.

I knew alters inside were having problems by their statements and questions so I tried my best to see what they were so upset about. After they explained what was bothering them, I found it easier to settle them down by relieving what they were so afraid of and letting them know that I would never put them in a situation again where I felt that they were in any kind of danger. I told them that if they could give me five minutes, I would see whether or not I felt it was safe to be there, and if they still did not feel safe we would leave.

Sometimes when I had a difficult time, some alters wanted something different while others were triggered and others were fine. It was challenging to try to make them satisfied. I often felt like a "mom" who can't please all of the "kids" with their individual demands. When I first started my healing process, I knew nothing of ministering to myself and particularly to alters inside of me. I was doing well to ignore them most of the time so I could do what I needed to do daily. I never thought to listen to their needs and what they were saying. Honestly, I hoped for so long that my mind was just making this all up and that they would eventually all go away, because I didn't know what to make of them. I kept thinking that if anyone else knew the perspective from inside my head they would have me put away forever.

Then, as my healing progressed, I eventually learned the alters I kept hearing inside of me were there to help. They helped keep me alive and from going crazy. This put a new perspective on them, and I now didn't have such distaste for them, but learned to accept them as ones who were really helping me all along. I figured that since I couldn't really get rid of them right away, I may as well learn to like them! So the process continued.

When one was desperately crying to leave a particular place, I would initially ignore her prior to understanding why she wanted to leave. As I continued to pay more attention to what they were saying, I learned that they always had a reason why they were saying something and why something may be bothering them. If an alter was mad because I was talking to someone she did not feel was safe for her, I learned to ask her questions about the situation. For example, I would ask, "What is it about that person that bothers you?" or "How did you feel when I was talking to that person?" or "Did that person remind you of anything?"

Usually in asking questions like these I was able to get answers from the alter that will determine what is really bothering her. For example, she may have answered back, "The person bothers me because they are wearing black around the neck and I don't like it when people wear black around the neck. It scares me." Or, "I felt scared and like I wasn't listened to when I wanted to leave that person. I felt like they were too close to me when you were talking to them. I felt afraid they would try to control me." If the person reminded the alter of anything, she may have said something like, "He was holding a black Bible and the man in the ritual was holding a black Bible, so I got scared. When the lady you talked to wanted to give you a hug, I remembered the cape lady who always smothered me." Or, "When she lifted her hands when she was praying for you, I was afraid of the power that would come and my not liking that power."

In a situation where I needed to talk to the same person again, though alters inside were extremely bothered, I learned to bargain with them. I wanted to acknowledge to the alters I heard them and listened to what they said. At the same time, I came up with a compromise where we could both be more comfortable. I didn't want to be in a situation that made them more uncomfortable. I didn't want to completely avoid things I needed to do as the core personality because an alter inside didn't like it and felt threatened or uncomfortable. At first, this was a tough balance.

It helped to know what they liked. For example, if one really liked ice cream and I was temporarily in an uncomfortable situation for her, I said to her, "I know that this may be difficult for you, but you can know that if anything becomes unsafe for us, we will leave. If we make it all the way through this hard situation for you, I will see that you have ice cream afterward."

This acknowledged she was going through a difficult time while I needed to do something. It also rewarded her for going through it without demanding we leave because it was too overwhelming. I also always gave them an out. By this I mean that the alter inside who is bothered didn't have to go for the bargain. If the situation became too hard for them, they just needed to tell me it was too hard for them and they needed to leave. Then I would leave.

Sometimes when this happened, I wanted them to know that I would continue to listen to how they felt about something but also wanted them to grow their trust. I would often encourage them by saying, "You have done so well up to this point. Is there any way you may be able to keep going and do great for five minutes longer?" I left the choice up to them; if they chose to stay for five minutes, I stayed for five minutes and asked again after the five minutes was up.

If they decided it was too scary still, I would leave. I wanted them to know they had a voice now, whereas before, they never did. I wanted to show them life is different now. Inside it may not seem different yet. In ministering to myself, I tried to come up with opportunities where they were faced with a choice and their decision would be backed by my actions. This helped to build their trust and propelled their healing.

Growing Up Backward

The baggage of a hurting person will inevitably inhibit her from growing emotionally and spiritually until the Lord heals her. How then does she get rid of the baggage that weighs her down, keeping her growth stunted? As it is important for someone to receive proper nutrition, get physical exercise and rest, learn how to relate in healthy attachments to grow physically and emotionally, it is equally important to receive these crucial elements in her healing. Many hurting people did not receive this growing up. What if the hurting person missed out on what she was supposed to receive emotionally and physically? How is it she can still gain what she needs in these areas where such deficits remain?

A hurting person was busy just trying to survive when all her abuse and trauma were taking place. The normal emotional and physical needs were not met during those critical years in childhood. As she is on her journey of healing it is important that we encourage her to learn how to "grow up backward." What do I mean by this?

Many people with DID have alters inside that are quite young, varying to older teenage years, to alters close to the person's age. It's like managing a lot of different people on the inside of your mind simultaneously. As with any babysitter with many people to watch, you may encounter those who don't get along with each other, arguments to break up, younger ones to bribe or compromise with, talking with younger ones about their fears and allowing them to enjoy younger activities, and so forth. This is important to remember as one with DID learns to grow up backward.

Several principles in particular have really helped me in this process of growing up backward. First, I have learned to give myself extra grace if I don't know how to do something. This has helped tremendously. In my journey, I often feared that if I don't do something exactly right, something bad will happen. A way I have learned to give myself more grace is by saying to myself, *If my life started in such a way where I did not have to fight for my life and I was able to live without the constant fear of death or awful scenarios, then I would have been able to learn this during that time. That was not the case. Now I can give myself the time to learn those things I wasn't able to focus on before.*

For example, social skills may be very poor among people who have DID. During the time that most children learn social and relational skills, we were spending that time trying to stay alive. Now I allow myself to intentionally observe lots of people and how they respond relationally. This has become a key in learning how to interact with people and what is normal in relationships.

Significant opportunities to learn this came when I lived with a Christian family. During this time, I was able to watch how they responded to each other, how they lived daily lives with each other, how they dealt with everyday life events, how they dealt with very difficult events, and how they interacted while under stress. Paradigms shifted in my mind about what healthy relationships looked liked. I never understood what a normal relationship in a family was until that time.

Another way I allow myself to grow up backward emotionally is by watching healthy children interact together. Because so much of a DID person's childhood was missed, it helps to see glimpses of a healthy childhood. Practical ways of doing this include visiting a park regularly and watching children play, especially with families, and how they interact together. Hear them laugh. Listen to their excitement as they are about to go down the slide. Watch their hair swing in the wind as they twirl on the tire swing. Smell the sand box as they build their imaginary castles and dream of wonderful kingdoms.

If it is helpful, encourage the hurting person to write her thoughts during her time at the park, uncensored. Not every thought may be happy. Perhaps she may experience sadness and grief as she sees what was supposed to be in her own life but wasn't. These thoughts and the acknowledgment of them are significant in her healing process as well.

Also, I allow myself to ask questions. I give myself grace to know it's alright if I do not already know or understand something. If my life had been lived like most people's, I would have known. The simple facts are that this wasn't the case. So I allow myself the time I need to learn these things now and not be so frustrated that I may look silly. Safe questions I have found to ask during times of *I should probably know this but I don't* are, "I'm sorry if I have missed the boat somewhere, but could you explain this?" or "This may sound stupid to you but I do not understand . . ." When questions such as these are prefaced with an *I am giving you a heads up that I don't know something,* it gives the other person the clue to give more grace in their answers. Most of the time, I have found questions like these work well.

Another way I allowed myself to grow up backward was to allow times for the younger ones inside to do things they enjoy. This gives those alters a space to grow emotionally as they were not able to before. Simple ways to do this are by asking younger alters what they like to do. Or, if you are a helper and working with a younger alter, knowing that alter's age is often a good indication of what she may like to do.

However, if that alter is not used to doing anything fun or enjoyable, she may not be able to tell you herself. An example of this is that I know I had several younger alters. How would I allow them to do something fun? One part I know of was five. What does a five-year-old girl like to do? This part liked to finger paint and work on her ABCs so that she can start learning how to read. She liked to color and be outside playing, to name a few activities. So, you may encourage the person to do any one of these things, allowing the alters inside to do them as well. They can also do age-appropriate things.

Something else I did to grow up backward was to allow alters inside to make choices they were never able to before. Also, this can aid in teaching alters about what safe choices are and what unhealthy choices are. An example of this is allowing an alter to pick out something she likes to eat at the grocery store. This is a safe choice for an alter to make.

The teaching comes into play when she is deciding what she wants to eat. Depending on what the alter decides about her snack, treat, or lunch, depends on how I helped her walk through the decision, as I am also aware of what she's saying inside. If a younger alter wants a sweet for lunch and that is all, I may compromise with her in the process of purchasing the sweet and say something to her inside like "How about we let another alter pick out a healthy lunch item and another alter a drink item, and you can have one sweet?" This way I was generally trying to listen and involve many alters in the process of lunch, as difficult and frustrating as one lunch meal may seem to be at times!

Another way to compromise if that alter does not agree may be to reward her in a different way by letting another alter make the choice. Finding something else we like that doesn't involve the lunch meal today is an option for the alter to still make a choice. An example of this is having a cartoon sticker on my hand all day long to look at, or something else simple they like often works.

There are times when not everyone inside will be happy despite efforts to please everyone on any given occasion. The goal in this whole process is to let the alters know you are listening to them and validating what they are telling you. Bribing and compromising sometimes works when this happens, but most of all what they are longing to know and see is they have a voice and are heard. When I couldn't do what they wanted and bribing didn't work, often I would simply say, "I hear what you are telling me. I want you to know you are being heard. This is what I hear you saying … Is there anything else you want to let me know about this? I am so glad you are talking about this. I want to know and hear everything you are feeling about this. I am so glad you feel safe enough to have a voice about this."

As much as possible I acknowledged them in this process. Much of the healing began when they were heard and validated no matter what they were talking about, whether it concerned a sweet at lunch or the pain they carried.

Questions to Consider

1. How is the Lord pursuing your heart to persevere in your journey?

2. In what ways are you different now than when you began your healing process? In what areas does He desire for you to "grow up backward" and learn what you missed out on?

3. How have you discovered God's perfect timing in your life?

4. How do you absorb truth in bite-sized pieces?

5. Ask the Lord to prepare your heart for integration and what, if anything, needs to happen in you before alters merge in your mind.

6. Be honest with the Lord about any fears you may have about alters integrating and ask Him how He desires to meet those concerns (i.e., loneliness, fear of not knowing how to be in situations the alters have always lived for you, etc.).

7. Write in your journal about His faithfulness in healing your mind and heart to this point.

Chapter 17

He Sets the Lonely in Families

God makes a home for the lonely; He leads out the prisoners into prosperity.

—Psalm 68:6

I WAS DRIVING with a friend who prayed consistently for me. She said, "Someone called the other day asking me if I knew anyone who needed a room to rent in exchange for taking care of animals and their house while they traveled. I thought of you." I was currently renting a room, but the idea of helping care for alpacas, dogs, a cat, and a turtle seemed fun. I liked the idea of getting to care for animals and not do horrible things. I thought maybe this was the way the Lord would redeem this area of my life. I loved animals. I wanted to be allowed to love them. I called the lady needing a boarder, but I didn't know what to expect.

We talked briefly and she had me over for dinner to meet them. I arrived late, embarrassed. *Now what are they going to think? Here I am late, great impression I am making, I am sure.* We sat around the island in the kitchen talking. Carrie had awakened from a nap after a busy day as a freshman in high school, and she started with cereal as an evening snack before dinner. Their cat came to greet me and ask for petting while "mom" explained the history of how they "adopted" the cat.

I already knew this family was different. They had love inside their house I had never known, and I didn't know what to think of it. The house was playing worship music in the background as we sat down for dinner starting with a salad followed by the main course. *They sit around the dinner table?* I didn't know what that was like. I was afraid I was going to mess up because I had never grown up sitting around a dinner table to eat. This was all new. I was afraid to let them know that I felt insecure as to what I was supposed to do. I had moved to the state a year earlier and they asked how I decided to move there. They talked about what they did, their family, and the various backgrounds of their lives. I was amazed they were willing to share all they had. They asked me what my background was, and I didn't know what to tell them. I had never been asked that question from people I hadn't known before.

Should I tell them? I briefly told them I had come from a background of abuse and believed I was walking a road of healing but didn't have far to go. They listened and made no judgments. They asked if they could talk with anyone who knew my story for a reference. The only person who knew was someone who believed she wouldn't have to deal with my background, as she thought I was almost all healed. They called her, and she told them, "There are just a few alters left inside, and there should be no issues." I was panicked at the thought of what they would do when they discovered I was still a wreck and far from being totally healed.

It didn't take long for them to discover how shattered I was, that I had Dissociative Identity Disorder, a background of SRA, and was still in need of great healing. There were nights I was afraid they would ask me to leave because they wouldn't want to deal with me. They realized when I wasn't able to pay rent several months in a row that my finances were as unstable as I was. They never asked me to leave because I wasn't able to pay. I didn't understand them. Anyone else would have asked me to leave. They had every right to do so. Instead they loved me and worked with me. They began ministering to alters inside. Every time alters began to speak, the family talked with them and loved them. They were never ashamed of them and never brushed them away.

Later, their older daughter graduated from college with plans to be married and go to medical school in the fall. She came home with her fiancé "Mitten," as the alters always called him. They unpacked bags, dirty laundry, and made their temporary home with us for the summer before heading to med school in a few months. I remember talking with "AppleDoc," another nickname by the alters, and thought, *Who is this girl?* I knew she was totally different from Carrie, her sister who I was used to living with by then. Later that year, Deidra (mom) flunked her mammogram and got tests back indicating she had breast cancer. We were devastated.

Unanswered questions and requests for prayer flooded to extended family, friends, and those we knew in our church families. Days were occupied with trying on wigs, chemo, surgeries, more chemo, weariness, and nights filled with prayer. A couple of days before a surgery Deidra agreed to go with me to a prayer session going through steps to freedom, hoping I would be free from much of what tormented me. Ten hours later there was relief in a few areas. I went as deep as I felt safe.

I knew my healing wasn't over and I still had much to confess, repent of, and come to the Lord with. I was afraid of exposing everything. I didn't want anyone to know the darkness I still had inside. I didn't tell what I was still a part of. I didn't want to release the control I believed I had. I wanted to believe that day's session was going to cover all my past and heal it all. The Lord's heart was to make me whole. My total healing didn't happen that day because of my own heart, not because of the Lord's. His timing is perfect. He knew I wasn't ready to be whole from all the SRA and trauma because my heart wasn't stable enough.

Week after week, Deidra fought breast cancer and the family rallied around her to come to wholeness. They continued to fight and rally around my healing also. I felt so undeserving of their love and support while Deidra was so sick. However, they continued to minister to me and the alters inside day and night. During this time I realized for the first time what it was to live life with a family who was safe. I learned safe families cry together and ask God hard questions together. This family taught me how to belong and be accepted.

They taught me how to set a table for dinner and how to prepare a meal. They taught me I could ask them any question, hard or easy, and it was invited. If they didn't know the answer, they told me; and we asked God together for wisdom and help. They taught me what can happen when they get upset and have hard days. They displayed being upset and still being totally safe.

I saw them have hard days many times. They never abused or threatened. They never left. They never called each other names to belittle one another. I watched them have disagreements and argue, and for the first time, I wasn't afraid when this happened. I knew I was still safe in the midst of an argument, and I didn't have to run away. No skillets would ever come toward my head because of their anger. I was totally safe.

AppleDoc and Mitten decided to stay for the year and hold medical school off for AppleDoc so they could be with Deidra. As AppleDoc and Mitten stayed, we had no idea how significant they also would be to my healing through the coming months. Even now, the family comments what they went through with me wouldn't have been possible without AppleDoc and Mitten also being there that year. The Lord knew what He was doing to have a family of six built around me at home to help me begin to heal. There were many memories the alters inside felt safer to share with AppleDoc and Mitten, and they related to them differently than others in the family.

Through those months they watched me struggle and try to find freedom. They watched me live with alters, and they learned what my life was really like with DID/SRA. They saw me have job after job, be sick time and time again, and wrestle with tormenting darkness. They watched me be contacted by others in darkness several times during this process and the devastations after being in contact with them by phone. I told the family about them wanting me to visit them out of state. My "adopted family" was upset I was thinking about going because they knew how much harm these people had on my life. They knew it was a scheme of the enemy to get me back and to give up trying to find freedom. They knew I was being manipulated again to operate under their control. They were adamant about it not being a good idea for me to go.

They prayed as I contemplated going. They prayed I would choose life, truth, and not go. They prayed I would see the trap I was stepping into. They prayed with a couple of others who were also ministering to me. I was warned that if I went, I would not be able to come back and live there because they didn't know what would happen to me while I was gone. They prayed this would be such a deterrent that I would choose not to go. I had so much to lose if I left. Though I was extremely unstable and broken still, my life since living there had already begun to change dramatically, and I was finally on a road to recovery. I finally knew a safe family and a place I could call home. I never had that before.

I didn't listen to their wisdom. I went out of state for two days and agreed to visit the others in darkness. The implications were devastating. I knew when I got back I needed to find another place to live. I knew I had made the wrong choice when I got on the plane. I had made one of the biggest mistakes of my life after all I had been given by my adopted family. I was afraid of losing their love and didn't really know what their response would be when I returned.

It wasn't worth the visit. I came back to my adopted family and cried about my mistakes and wished so badly I hadn't lived the last few days out of state because of what took place. I wished I had listened to their wisdom, their truth, and what they believed was best for me. I was so ashamed about what happened, I initially lied to them about part of what took place while I was gone. I was reeling to try to make my mistakes better, but instead I made them worse by not being truthful with them. In a bigger mess, they still loved me and never abandoned me.

They kept to their word, and I needed to find another place to live. They knew I had made a choice even though I regretted it deeply. I moved into an apartment shortly after. I will never forget when they agreed to come over and pray over me and the apartment for the Lord's safety and presence to protect me in my new place. They prayed for mercy and grace over me in spite of my many mistakes. I didn't realize how committed they were to me. I thought I had lost their love because I didn't deserve it after what I had done.

They still pursued a relationship with me. After I had moved out they still invited me to be a part of family events, holidays, and included me as their family. At first I thought it was just because they knew I was alone and would need people to hang out with on various holidays. This was true, but I had no idea how much they really loved me as part of their family until years later. I continued to be in contact with them through various job changes, different apartments, and different educational pursuits—attempts to find freedom and healing.

I was having coffee with a friend one day, and she was talking about wanting to be married and to start that portion of her life. I panicked inside. My friend still had her father to walk her down the aisle, a mother who would help pick out her wedding dress, and a sister to be a bridesmaid. I kept thinking, *Who would be those safe people for me on my wedding day?* I was afraid of not having an answer and didn't know if my adopted family would be willing to fill those roles in my life. I didn't know the extent to which they were committed to being my family or if my time with them was just a safe year, not necessarily my new family but a safe family I would forever cherish.

I wasn't sure what their role was in my life anymore. One night, driving back to my adopted family's house, with tears streaming down my face, I wondered if they were to be my new family forever. Months before, the Lord had asked me to sever ties with my birth family. I had done so and asked Him to confirm what I had heard from Him. I asked Him to provide a safe family for me, who would forever be part of my life. I needed a family I could be with, live life with, and grow old with as the Lord saw fit. I had no idea if the family who became my adopted family was to be this family, or if the Lord would have another family to fill this role in my life.

I came home to my adopted family and they knew something was wrong. It didn't take much for them to realize something was wrong when I was upset. We all sat in the living room, and I blurted out through sobs that I didn't know if they thought I was a part of their family forever or if I was just another girl who lived with them who happened to be broken and was ministered to by them. I told them I was afraid that if I ever walked down an aisle to be married I wouldn't know who would be by my side to give me away to my husband. I told them I was afraid if I were to ever bear another child, who would be next to me, helping me through? I didn't know if they were my family or if they wanted to commit to that role in my life. I told them I didn't know if they loved me that much. They all said, "Yes! We are your family. Yes, we love you that much! Yes, we are with you forever." "Dad" told me how honored he would be to walk me down an aisle one day and how much he looked forward to such an amazing, exciting part of my life.

They exclaimed their love and commitment to me in ways I had never heard. I was overwhelmed at their responses. I couldn't believe how much they loved and cared for me. I knew then I belonged as part of their family, and I could call them my family for keeps. I knew I would always have a safe home to come to wherever they were in the world. I knew they loved me as their own daughter, and the Lord had set me in a family where my heart had been so lonely. He came to fill the lonely chasms inside.

Questions to Consider

1. Ask the Lord to fill any loneliness you may have and how He desires to fill all your empty places with His hope, perfect love, and complete provision.

2. Ask the Lord if there is unforgiveness in your heart you need to take ownership for concerning anyone. Ask Him specifically about those who have hurt you growing up and those in your life now. Tell the Lord how they hurt you and ask Him to take each of those circumstances and place them on the cross, never to be held against your heart again. Though difficult, make the choice to forgive each person and place their sins on the cross, surrendering everything to the Lord, and allow Him to remove all the pain.

3. Ask the Lord to forgive you and remove the sin in your heart. Ask Him if there is any area in your life you haven't wanted to come to Him about concerning hurt in your heart. Write down what He speaks in truth over these areas.

4. As you make the choice to forgive all those who have hurt you, also make the choice to forgive yourself. The Lord

has mercy and unfailing love over each of us. His love and forgiveness can cleanse us!

5. Ask the Lord how He desires to expand your heart and/or family to "adopt" one who is broken and in need of a safe, loving, godly family to help minister to them.

6. What is the Lord asking you concerning your church family? What is your place in your local church family and what areas is the Lord challenging you to step into within your local church?

7. Who is your family? How might the Lord want to transform your life if you allow Him within the safe family He provides for you?

Chapter 18

Crossroads to Freedom

—◈◊◈—

DURING ONE EDUCATIONAL pursuit of getting a masters degree in counseling, I was fortunate to have small classes and professors who took individual interest in their students to encourage them and pray over them. In a couple of these classes, one particular professor taught a class on grief and loss and another on Post Traumatic Stress Disorder (PTSD). I thought I was taking them because she was highly respected in her field and the classes fulfilled part of the requirement for my degree. The Lord had a whole new thing coming for me! It didn't take long for me to come face to face with the reality of what my life was really like before I lived in that geographical state, now in safety.

Her homework was intense, having me list in detail all the grief and loss I had encountered throughout my life. I had no idea how much was there. I will never forget writing a cute list of the common things I was alright with remembering, and wanting to be done with the assignment. The next part was to pick the top ten and write about each one and why they were significant enough to be in the top ten. I thought I had done my assignment well, my notebook paper neatly filled with a list of fifteen losses and why I thought I had grieved over them. I thought my homework was done. Piece of cake. I could move on to other agendas for the evening.

But I wasn't done. The Lord wouldn't let go of my heart as He kept nudging it, asking me if I wanted to engage with the assignment and allow Him to work through her homework and heal me. I didn't know. I was afraid of the answers if I asked Him about my losses. I avoided the homework, fearful of what would happen if I were real about the questions my teacher proposed. Each loss the Lord brought to my mind was painful but came with healing. I made a decision in those classes to be real and allow the Lord to expose the pain and the memories associated with all my losses.

He didn't heal me overnight, but He healed in His perfect timing as I continued to discover I could trust Him in the process. During the semester I confided in my teacher about memories I was having and asked for prayer on numerous occasions whenever I struggled. I learned during those courses that I was too broken to continue the masters program. The intensity of processing involved with no one to consistently help me with trauma that surfaced was difficult. I had several around me who deeply cared for me, but each one encouraged me to find help somewhere else, help they couldn't provide.

I began to ask the Lord to provide someone to work with me and alters inside, such as a counselor or mentor at a church. I needed someone who would understand my background of DID/SRA. I decided to let go of the masters program and take a break to pursue medical interests. I realized what I needed to pursue was healing. Where? I had no idea.

I started school and a different job related to the medical field and both fell flat. In a new city with no friends, with difficult books to study, I saw how deeply broken I still was. I cried out to the Lord to help me find someone or a church who would know how to help me. I was suicidal all over again. My nightmares were constant again. My memories mocked me daily, and I didn't know how to get rid of them or deal with them without the support of my adopted family. I knew I was going downhill fast and needed help.

I asked my professor what church she went to and if she knew of anyone who could work with me consistently. She gave me the name of her church that had a prayer ministry. I followed up with the prayer ministry and met with the lady who led the ministry. I wrote her a letter explaining what I needed help with and my background of DID/SRA. I figured she would either know what I was talking about and lead me in the right direction or look at me as though I were crazy and have no idea what to tell me. I would be no worse off either way. She read the letter and knew exactly what I was talking about. I had never been so relieved in my life! She got it. She understood where I was coming from and what I would need. She told me someone had lived with her for five years with my background and she had watched her come into healing and wholeness. I couldn't believe what I was hearing.

She told me she was not the one to help me, but she knew of a couple about an hour away who might be able to work with me as they previously ministered to those with DID/SRA. She didn't know it, but I had moved fifteen minutes away from where this couple's church was just days before. She told me their names and the church they were pastors of. She had no idea what was to come as I began to go to that church. I came to know this church as an additional safe family in my life. People in the church loved God and loved me before they knew me. I didn't understand why. I hadn't done anything to deserve the love they showed me in my first weeks of attending.

I was an hour away from my adopted family when I started school in a medical specialty. I thought attending the school was the reason I moved to where I was. That was the initial hook the Lord used to get me where I needed to be geographically, but little did I know the real reason at that point. The real reason He had me there was to be healed. I was fifteen minutes away from the church He wanted for me. I didn't know this when I moved. He just had fun leading me, letting me discover how close I was to the church and the healing He would have for me. This was the place where I would journey out of the darkness into complete life and wholeness.

Jesus is sovereign in how He chooses to heal any of us. In my journey, what became necessary was being in an intense, spiritually activated, alive church that was fully engaged to see those in bondage set free. While in this church, the Lord provided a safe church family, and this is when the majority of my healing happened.

The second Sunday I was there, a lady shared her testimony as part of the service how the Lord had rescued her from a background of Satanic Ritual Abuse and healed her from Dissociative Identity Disorder. I was sitting against the back wall of the church and nearly fell out of my chair at what I was hearing! I had never heard anyone share "my story" anywhere, much less in front of the whole church. Church, as I knew it, was often a place where more abuse took place. I became faintish and didn't know what was happening inside of me as I continued to listen to her story. She shared of some of her horrific memories and what she walked through to get out of her torment and darkness. She talked about how the Lord had come to set her free and heal her. She said ministry at the church had helped her heal in ways she had never known. I still couldn't grasp and believe all I was hearing.

I felt as though I was in a dream too good to be true. I wanted so desperately to know a place and people who could help me heal as she did but didn't know if that would ever be a reality. When she finished sharing the miraculous things the Lord had done in her life, everyone in church stood on their feet and hooted and hollered for what the Lord had done. What was happening? This was no dream. This was real. I wanted it to be real for me also. Was I really in the right place at the right time? Had the Lord really led me there for healing? I knew at that instant my move to that city had nothing to do with my educational pursuits or new job but everything to do with His placing me in that church, for my total healing.

When the service was over, I went up to the pastor and told him I needed to meet Tom and Diane. He told me, "I'm Tom, and this is my wife here, Diane." I told them I was referred there by Lynn, who told me they used to work with those with DID/SRA. Diane asked where I was in my journey. I didn't know what to tell her. I had thought I was much further along than where I realized I was. I knew I was very broken but was afraid to tell her. I told her I had been working on healing for years but still had a ways to go. I felt that was a safe answer.

She pierced through my answer and told me about the church and what they did. She told me that there are so many who want help, but they only work with those who attend there regularly. She asked me if I wanted to meet Lindsey, who had shared her testimony just moments before. I was overwhelmed by what I had heard and declined. I knew if I stayed at the church I would meet her soon enough.

Weeks went by and I had lunch at the church every Sunday, discovering the family in this church was unlike any other I had known. One Sunday I happened to sit next to Lindsey's kids and husband, having no idea they were who they were. A few moments later Lindsey sat at the same table with her family and introduced herself to me. I couldn't believe I ended up sitting at her table. I quickly shared with her how I appreciated her sharing her story because I had never heard anyone share "my story." I was so grateful I knew one other person who would know what my life was like and if healing was possible. Now I knew it was. I saw her. I saw she was different from what life is like in the horror. I saw her interacting with her husband and kids and knew the Lord must have healed her. I knew the Lord must have transformed her mind and heart even by the way she talked so normally that Sunday afternoon at the lunch table.

She asked where I was from. I told her. She was taken aback, and I didn't know why until she told me that she also grew up in that state. She asked where I grew up. I told her. She was surprised again as we realized moments later we had grown up five miles apart from each other, living very similar lives of darkness and horror. I realized again the Lord's amazing hand to lead us *both* to the same place to be free and healed, finally! What an amazing God we have! He is so intimately acquainted with the details of our lives and knows exactly what needs to happen for His whole healing to take place in us. For me, this was part of the healing process. She became part of my safe spiritual family at church. I belonged there. I was accepted there. No one ever judged me or condemned me. They embraced me and began to pray for my total freedom.

I continued to attend there and discovered different aspects of healing that God wanted to do in me in the Sunday services. He moved and healed as long as I stepped out of darkness and surrendered my mind, will, and emotions to Him. He never failed to run to me with more of His healing when I merely brushed forward at times. Through the weeks and months I met with Diane and Lisa, another prayer minister, while they watched the Lord do His incredible works of healing, deliverance, and restoration. I knew I was safe during those appointments. I knew the Lord had also placed them as part of His family in my life. They loved me. They cared and prayed for me before they met me as they had been in prayer for the Lord to let those with DID/SRA come and find safety, freedom, and wholeness in Him as part of that church. He answered and led me there.

I didn't know what would be exposed while I was part of this safe church. I didn't want them to know the darkness I was still involved in. I knew in order to break away completely from all my deception, secrets, and schemes of the enemy over me I would have to repent of everything. I was fearful that everything I ever did associated with the enemy would be exposed. I didn't know how they would respond once they realized I was still being used as a tool of the enemy, even though some alters of my heart wanted freedom. However, not all the alters were on board to pursue healing and freedom for months after I started meeting consistently for prayer and healing sessions.

The alters inside needed to know who God was first. He showed them alright. In incredible ways the Lord continued to expose His love and mercy, causing the others to stand amazed at how specifically the Lord knew how to be with each of them. As more alters discovered the truth of His heart for them, the enemy wanted to convince them they would always belong to darkness. Satan didn't win. Though the enemy continued to try to use alters as secret weapons to cause destruction in the lives of people at my church, he was exposed. God exposed the enemy's work of darkness and rescued the alters inside for His Kingdom and purposes.

During this process, I was encouraged by Diane and Lisa to search my heart for what it really desired: freedom or captivity. They never judged me or gave up working with me in the midst of difficult instances that happened in the church as a result of my brokenness and decisions related to darkness. I kept wondering why they didn't give up on me, even after all my sin. Instead, they, and others from the prayer team, continued to intercede on my behalf. They sought the Lord for my freedom and wholeness when I didn't deserve healing after what they knew I had done.

I did want freedom. I was willing to do whatever freedom cost. I made difficult decisions to break away from all darkness. I severed ties with all those who I still participated in darkness with. I renounced and confessed my sin to the Lord and, when appropriate, to Diane and Lisa. Total repentance was absolutely required. I knew I couldn't hide anything or hold anything back from the Lord if I were to be completely healed and free. This process took several months.

Also during this time, the Lord continued to reveal Himself as I attended a Bible class the church provided. I began to consistently read His Word and meditate specifically on verses others in the church were also reading that day. I started writing in my journal about what God was speaking to me. Common themes were His love, who He is, who I am, my role in His Kingdom Church, gifts He gave me, sin, repentance, and His sacrificial work on the cross.

Another night of the week a "healing place" was offered for those who wanted prayer for any kind of healing. Many were healed every week. I went nearly every week. At first I didn't like anyone other than Diane or Lisa to pray for me. I didn't trust others in the church. I went for prayer a couple of times. I was fearful and disrespectful of them. I told them they wouldn't understand me. I blew off their encouragement and prayer and acted as though it wasn't helpful. I was ashamed. Alters inside were upset. Other alters were confused. Others were angry, feeling I was taking advantage of something that could potentially help. The Lord spoke to me clearly about how I treated them and my need for repentance. I was asked after this not to go for prayer until I was receptive to what they had heard from the Lord on how to minister to me.

I didn't know how they would respond to me when I told them I needed healing from the "voices in my head," or from the darkness I always felt inside, or from despair. Throughout the weeks of just praying upstairs with the worship service taking place, I knew I needed wholeness even if I was fearful of what others would think. During one particularly difficult week, I crossed over from my feelings of fear and decided to open my heart to receive what the prayer teams would minister. I took a risk. God never failed me. I told the leader of the prayer teams

I really did want freedom and repented for how I had behaved. They graciously allowed me to receive prayer again. Almost every week I went for prayer. When I didn't, I spent time in worship, seeking the Lord on my own. He never failed me then either. He constantly met me and ministered to my soul when I sought Him.

Weeks passed. I was beginning to notice bits of progress. I realized that, little by little, my heart was changing. My mind was getting quieter. My life was becoming a series of choices about seeking after truth rather than defaulting into dark patterns. Month after month, I continued to meet with Diane and Lisa, and the Lord continued to move in greater ways on my behalf, setting alters free. His work was spectacular. I didn't walk away every time excited for what He was asking of me. But I did walk away knowing He had met with me, even when His questions for me were difficult. He required all of my heart to break away for freedom.

I gave Him all of my heart. At this point, after months of ministry and the Lord meeting me, His accelerated work in my heart was changing the very core of who I was. This was the turning point. I had come from wondering if I would ever be whole and healed to knowing now it really was possible. It was just a matter of His sovereign timing as I continued to seek Him with everything inside me. He was asking me to increase my intensity for Him. I began to worship Him like never before. I cried out to Him like never before. I sought His truth like never before. I wrote in my journal what I heard Him speaking and asked Him questions I never dared ask Him before. A few months later, I knew total healing was close. He was undeniably coming to heal my heart as I chased after Him.

While I was chasing Him and He was coming to me, different ones in the church began to love me in ways I will never forget. One day when I was struggling with tormenting thoughts, an artist, who I will call Renee, gave me a journal during service.

She had painted the cover of the journal beautifully with a message only the Lord and I knew the significance of. She didn't really know me, but the Lord let her know what I needed and she loved me. She gave me the journal that evening with fresh pages to declare the truth of who I am in Christ.

I began to write my new identity in Him in those new pages along with the truth I chose to believe to rid me of my tormenting thoughts. She had no idea what that journal meant to me. I had just finished my last one, and I wanted to start afresh but was afraid of journaling more pages of defeat. I had written in journals my whole life but only of darkness, defeat, and longings to be free. I had not yet written a journal filled with pages of the hope, life, and healing that He would do in me, until she gave me this journal.

I knew this was a different journal to use for my significant time of healing. This journal was part of my healing process in ways she will never know. I poured out my heart before the Lord in that journal like none other, and He has poured His heart over me in those pages. The more I wrote to Him, the more He came and continued to heal. Full freedom was on its way.

Questions to Consider

1. If you were to receive a journal from the Lord, what questions would you have for Him?

2. To complete the other five questions for this chapter, write five questions you believe He would have for you.

Chapter 19

Learning What Normal Is

⁓⁂⃝

I AM STILL learning what "normal" is. I had lived life not knowing what that meant in many areas of daily life. As I look back on how different my life is compared to how it was, some areas seem funny to me now. I weep with joy and gratitude at the faithfulness of our God. As I remember how my life was I am constantly reminded how He truly pulled my life from the pits of darkness. I could give many examples revealing what I missed out on and what the Lord has restored in those places of deficit. I will mention a few, only to give indications of basics of life I didn't know. I didn't even realize what I didn't know until the Lord made a way for me to learn them in safe places with people.

I didn't know some basics of hygiene. I tried to watch how everyone took care of themselves. I pretended I knew exactly what to do. I felt I should have known and was embarrassed on many occasions when I felt such a blank place inside of me for not knowing. I played on a volleyball team when I was older. One day, in a volleyball match, my team was losing by eight points. My coach was frustrated as each volley did not favor our scoreboard. She called a time out and lectured as any coach would, stating that part of the reason we were losing so badly was because we weren't calling the ball whenever we wanted to send the sailing ball back. She exclaimed, "It's just what you do. Calling the ball is as normal and common as changing your underwear every day!" My team laughed at how serious she stated this and at the analogy everyone immediately related to. I was caught not laughing but thinking, *You are supposed to change your undergarments every day?* I had no idea. From that day on, I changed my undergarments daily.

I learned a lot while playing on sports teams. Little did they know how many basic things in life I learned in volleyball matches. I never told anyone the basics I was learning at various stages of healing. I didn't want to be embarrassed when I didn't know things they had learned growing up in a reasonably normal life. I kept my newfound discoveries between the Lord and me. He knew what I didn't know. I trusted He would teach me everything I needed in His timing. He is still teaching me.

Another time I will always remember that brought me to a level of normalcy was when I was with a friend in a restaurant. I was trying to contain my excitement, because I didn't want her to know I had never been to a restaurant or ordered food from a menu before. I was in college. My friend acted like this was old hat for her, and she asked me if I knew what looked good. I was honestly overwhelmed at the busy people walking around and the waiters frantically trying to do their jobs. Platters of food and cups full of drinks on platters above peoples' heads looked as though they were ready to fall on many occasions. The smells of different foods, the sounds of clatter in the background of dishes being served, and everyone talking around us was more than I imagined it would be. It wasn't bad. I just was experiencing something brand new while trying not to let my friend know. I just wanted to be normal, knowing how to go to eat in a restaurant with a friend without prior instructions.

Our waiter came by with a scribble pad and asked us what we wanted. I had no idea. The menu was a book with more options than I knew what to do with. My friend was ready to order, and then it was my turn. I told the waiter I couldn't decide so he came back later. Thirty minutes later, after my friend figured out that I was having difficulty knowing what to pick, I decided. I finally told her I didn't know how to order. I remember asking her if I should just name the item or should I tell the waiter the number? I didn't know how it worked. I didn't know if you paid right then when the waiter came or later. I didn't know if you could ask for seconds. I had no idea what going out to eat was like.

The waiter came back and my friend said, "Tell him what you want and they will bring it out when it's ready. They will bring out a drink before the meal, so would you like a drink also?" I was relieved she was showing me the ropes of ordering food. I was also proud that I did something new, something part of normal life I could now enjoy, not feeling so stupid trying to figure it out. My friend never made fun of me for what I didn't know. I eventually got better at deciding what food to order.

I remember the first time I had to do laundry by myself. Everyone around me knew what to do. They were separating their clothes into different piles. At first I thought they must be sorting the cleanest to the dirtiest. But I learned fast when I did laundry by myself that they were separating them by colors. My first loads didn't come out from dryers the same colors they went in. I quickly learned how to separate whites from colors before having to get a new wardrobe. Whew! I didn't know how much soap to put in, or where, and had no idea what cycle to put the machines on. Everything was new to me. I guessed. Wrong. I put too much soap in, and before I knew it, the cycle was spilling soapsuds from the edges of the lid and beginning to cover the linoleum floor. What began to be a bubble bath for the floor became an adventure of trying to clean the mess before anyone walked in and asked what happened. Fortunately, the spare towels that had not fit in the washer were available to mop up the soapsuds. I didn't know if I should turn the washer off or if I should let the cycle run its course. I didn't know if the suds would keep pouring out of the lid. Finally, the lid popped open from the pressure, and the cycle stopped. That answered my question! I took the clothes out and put them in my hamper wet and extremely soapy from my guessing game. I knew I had to ask someone for assistance because the machine needed attention at that point. I was embarrassed. I wanted to tell them the machine malfunctioned, rather than "I have never done laundry before and didn't know how much soap to put in the machine." I told them the machine needed attention.

I took the wet clothes to my place because I was overwhelmed at the thought of attempting laundry again. The next day I was greeted by lovely smells of mildew because the wet clothes sat overnight in my hamper. I didn't know when you left something wet for a long period of time it would mildew. Again, I learned something new and discovered mildew smell was difficult to get out. Eventually, I learned the basics of laundry. Ironing? That came much later!

I remember when I lived with a roommate, knowing nothing on how to cook. She didn't know this and figured anyone my age would know the basics of cooking. One night when she was getting a dinner together and I hadn't lived there long, she asked me to put some water on the stove to get it ready for pasta. I didn't know she was asking me to put water on to boil. I put water in a pot and put it on the stove. I didn't know what kind of heat to put the stove on, or how to boil water. I didn't know what water looked like when it boiled. She was confused at first that I really didn't know how to boil water. She taught me. She told me she didn't realize how much I had missed out on growing up. Situations such as learning the basics of cooking and being in the kitchen made me feel I would not be hopeless anymore. She also had grace to teach me, as many others did in my journey.

Learning the basics of life got easier, as anything does the more it is attempted. The more I did something, the more I got the hang of it, and the more fun it became to do. I learned to give myself some grace when I didn't know stuff others knew. I continually had to remind myself that they grew up doing these things. I grew up learning how to survive horror. Their lives weren't like mine, or they may have struggled also. When I remembered this, it was easier to allow myself to learn something everyone else already knew.

Another time I remember driving in the city where I had recently moved. It was the first city I had been in where I often didn't know where I was directionally. I remember wanting to go to a friend's house for the evening but panicking because I didn't know how to follow streets or directions to her house. I didn't know how to read a map. I almost cancelled our plans because the idea of trying to figure out how to drive myself there overwhelmed me to tears. I hated always feeling like I didn't know how to do something. I wanted to know the basic things everyone else knew. Everyone else my age knew how to follow street directions and get places when they weren't familiar with new territory.

I called my friend and told her my dilemma of being afraid of driving because I didn't want to get lost and miss out on our evening. She repeated her directions for me, thinking she must not have made them clear. They were perfectly clear. I just didn't know how to get from point A to point B with directions or a map. I finally had to explain to her I had never driven to a new place before. I expected her to think I was stupid and give up on our plans and not want to spend time with someone who didn't know simple things in life.

My friend didn't respond like I expected. The Lord was so good to provide me with gracious friends. She offered to come to my place, have me drive, while she took the passenger seat and taught me how to follow street directions. On one turn she took me down a wrong road on purpose to get me to use a map. She showed me where we were and where we wanted to be. I learned. She had me try to find the rest of the way there without her assistance, available to help in case I took another wrong turn. We made it! I walked in her house proud that I had accomplished a minor learning curve of driving. We celebrated with a funny movie and a dinner she had already made.

There were countless times after that incident that I drove to new places. There were too many times to count of times I was really lost. But I got better. Whenever I arrived late, my friends usually knew it was because I got lost. I was known for it. Later, I started arriving on time. I began to learn my way around and places became more familiar. I learned street names and where I was in the city. I didn't feel so overwhelmed anymore. I learned how to ask for help when I had no idea where to go next. I learned how to carry local maps in my car when traveling.

Now, driving places no longer overwhelms me. The Lord has allowed this place of difficulty in my life as a place of fun. Now, I enjoy taking drives and long road trips to places I have never been. I told a friend recently of a trip I took several years ago. She knew of my prior difficulty with driving. She suddenly exclaimed, "You went by yourself, and you weren't afraid?" She couldn't believe I had learned and grown to such an extent in that area of my life. It took three days to get to where I was headed. I only got lost a couple times but not badly. I knew then how to follow maps and had a great time. I knew my life was becoming more normal.

Another area of normalcy I came to learn was developing normal conversation skills. I was with my adopted family having dinner, and they were each talking about their day. Their talk of what happened at work, about the dog needing to get something checked out at the vet, and varieties of salad dressings on the table was a new dynamic of conversation that I wasn't used to. I didn't know how to participate in table conversations. I stayed quiet, fearing I wouldn't ever know what to say. I wanted to talk, but I didn't know if it mattered.

A drastic change in healing caused me to realize that my words do matter. Even if they are words describing a recipe I liked or what kinds of vegetables grow well in the garden, I learned my words were important. I learned I mattered as they listened to my words even when I didn't know how to engage well in conversation. I thought the only things worth talking about were life-and-death scenarios. That was all I knew. I thought that unless it was a memory, a serious spiritual matter, or other heavy content it wasn't worth spending the energy to talk about. Heavy, spiritual, horrific memories were all my mind rehearsed and knew to talk about after I discovered it was safe.

As a result, I didn't carry conversations with people well if they involved any other topic. I didn't know how to have friends without submarine diving into the relationship. It wouldn't take long into the friendship for me to overwhelm them with my brokenness. I didn't know how to be a friend without prematurely saying, "Hi, my name is Joy, and I am a Satanic Ritual Abuse survivor." Not in exactly those words, but in effect. This was the extent to which I overwhelmed someone. I didn't know how to relate with people on healthy terms without diving into territory they didn't want to know about initially.

We spent a lot of time around the dinner table at my adopted family's house. On one occasion, we were with others and an eight-year-old relative was struggling with the conversation. She wanted to talk about topics not related to what were being discussed. I heard Deidra explaining, "It's like putting the pieces of a puzzle together or a pie. Each person has something to contribute to the conversation happening. You say your piece of the pie and let others talk about it with your piece added now." Something clicked inside of me right as she said this. I felt I just got what I needed to build stones of meaningful conversation that all could take part in. I learned to recognize what the topic was and how to stay on topic and ask questions about what was being shared. I learned that most topics discussed are not life-and-death matters and that this was normal. I learned topics not related to horror, deep spiritual issues, or various kinds of trauma could be discussed, and it's healthy to engage with lighter areas of life also. The more I learned to engage in lighter conversation, the more I learned it was safe to let my soul rest. My soul no longer required the intensity of conversation it was so used to. My soul wasn't afraid anymore. I was learning how to engage in normal conversation. Communication in relationships became much easier and friendships more healthy as a result.

My nights were becoming more and more restful rather than nights of nightmares or horror. My days were becoming days where I was fully awake because I had begun to sleep through entire nights like never before. My time was becoming more filled with hours I could totally account for, versus hours an alter lived.

My life was changing, and I was learning so much about how He continued to restore every shattered place in my life. I didn't know when this would take place but was confident He was healing me. I knew I had much to learn in the stages of healing I was walking in. He was teaching me. He was changing me. I was learning what normal was in my life. I began to love the new normal He had for me.

Questions to Consider

1. What are areas in your life that everyone else seems to have learned, but you haven't?

2. What have you believed about yourself because you haven't learned those areas?

3. Write in your journal about those areas. Ask the Lord for truth about who you are in Him when you have areas in your life that are "blank spots."

4. Ask the Lord how to be intentional about areas you want to learn but haven't known how to begin.

5. Pick one area. Repent for word curses and criticism you have spoken over yourself. Repent for any lies you believed about yourself.

6. Allow the Lord to bring opportunities in your life so that you have choices to engage in these areas you never have before. When you engage in these new opportunities, write about them.

7. What fears might you have in trying new things? Ask the Lord to show you how to combat fear in your heart and choose to fight with truth.

Chapter 20

Living Whole, Healed, and Liberated

I AM SITTING on a swing at church, eating an ice cream cone with the Lord. We are celebrating what happened. He did it! He healed me. He healed every alter inside of me and brought them into my wholeness. Totally. He left no part of my life unchanged. He healed my body physically from all abusive damage. He healed all trauma and destruction in my body and my soul. Every physical ailment I struggled with for years is totally gone. Each emotional trauma and memory has been replaced with His healing. My mind is restored and whole. I had known for months during the intensity of the healing process that the Lord had yet to heal me of particular memories from the satanic rituals. I asked the Lord to heal me completely. In His perfect, sovereign timing He did. Until then, I kept believing He would.

I did what I knew to do during this time, the basics. I continued to read and declare the Scriptures and aggressively prayed truth over my life. I interceded in warfare against the enemy as curses from the enemy continued to be thrown against me. I stayed steady in the basics of attending church nearly every time the doors were open. I gave the Lord any opportunity He wanted to come and make Himself known to me. Not all these times seemed life changing, but they were.

They were life changing even when I didn't realize what was happening because I knew the Lord wasn't leaving me the same way each time I encountered Him and His presence. Each meeting softened alters inside to receive Him completely. Each time opened the door for Him to move further on my behalf as He saw my desire for complete freedom. Each time I worshipped the Lord in spirit and in truth, doors were opened from Him to reveal Himself in greater ways to me. As we worship He begins to open our eyes to complete truth and revelation from Him of who He is and desires to be in us. I believed Him.

I believed He would heal me in His perfect timing. I believed He would reveal what I needed to do for complete freedom. I knew I was drastically different than when I began the healing process, but I also knew it wasn't yet completed. One week in particular I had an unusual sense in my heart that the time for complete healing and freedom was getting very close. I had no idea when the time would be but knew it was imminent.

I began to seek the Lord more during this time. I asked Him to prepare my heart for whatever He desired. A couple weeks later a guest speaker who has a healing ministry, Joan Hunter, was coming to our church. I previously had plans for that weekend and hadn't planned on going to the conference. I realized the Lord was speaking to me about my total healing coming close, and the night prior to the conference the Lord began to speak to me about needing to go. I didn't have any idea why.

I wasn't even going to "get healing," but to allow the Lord another opportunity to do whatever He wanted to do in me. I just wanted Him and knew as I sought Him in every opportunity, my healing and freedom would be a natural byproduct because He is the Great Physician and Wonderful Counselor. I gave Him as many open doors as I could. The Lord saw me. He met me in ways I had never known before. He completely healed and set me free from every remaining remnant of my shattered soul. He did it miraculously.

It happened in the Saturday afternoon portion of the conference. Joan Hunter was talking about breaking off word curses, making renunciations concerning sin in our past, and other areas pertaining to our hearts. I remember wondering how much trauma still remained in my heart as she discussed how trauma was a root in many physical struggles. I knew there was still trauma held in my heart needing healing. I knew I needed Him to heal me and integrate alters remaining inside still tied in ropes of bondage. Memories of those in darkness flashed in my mind's eye of various traumas related to SRA and began to stir in my heart. She asked if there was anyone in the room who would get physically ill or sick if they saw a particular person they knew come in the room.

I knew right then she was talking to me as I had just been thinking about those involved with the horror I knew. I knew then if I were to see any one of them walk into the room I would have gotten physically ill and run out. I knew she was talking about me. My heart pounded in my chest and I began to sweat. I had no idea what was about to happen. I hoped healing was on His agenda! I knew I needed to raise my hand, as that question pertained to me directly.

I raised my hand and she saw me and asked me to come forward. My heart was shaking like a leaf, and I was nervous being in front of everyone there. However, I was determined to do whatever it took to get free. In front of everyone, gut honesty and vulnerability made room for Him to do what He does best: heal and set free! She asked me a few questions relating to those I was thinking about when I raised my hand, and I answered. She stated she was going to do something she had never done before. She stated she had a picture in her mind about my being tied up in ropes like a mummy, from head to toe in bondage. She saw me all tied up, tight in bondage. I was stunned.

Little did she know this was a reality in my life as part of Satanic Ritual Abuse. She had no idea what my background was. She knew nothing of my trauma. She knew nothing of my past, who I was, or my healing process. She did not know that what the Lord showed her was exactly one of the memories I had the week before she came. I was in need of healing from these last memories the Lord was exposing. God exposes things in us for the purpose of allowing Him to heal us. She had no idea these were the last of the memories I was dealing with. I had been only dealing with the Lord about those particular memories.

When she told me what she saw and I knew she saw my particular memories of SRA, I was convinced the Lord came just for me and the last alters who needed healing. He made a show of healing just for them. He called me up to the front for healing, just for the last alters inside crying out for freedom. As they continued to cry inside, "Let me out, let me out of this cage and break the ropes off of me!" I knew He had heard us. We were all going to get totally healed right then.

The Lord cared and loved me to the extent of showing that memory to someone else so I could be healed and set free. I knew then the Lord wanted me there that weekend and the word He spoke to me that my healing was "very close" was right before my eyes. She stated that the Lord was going to have her squeeze me to imitate briefly the ropes that were wrapped around my entire body. Then she asked the Lord to heal me from all the trauma, pain, grief, loss, betrayal, despair, oppression, and every way the enemy was binding me to keep me from doing what I was created to do. She let me go as the Lord unraveled all the ropes around me. He physically unraveled every last one of them in my soul and from all the alters needing freedom.

He loosed me out of that cage to total freedom. I knew He had completely set me free. I knew my heart was whole from all the years of pain and horror related to SRA. She also prayed for my purity and my body that had been specifically damaged through the years of abuse. I didn't tell her anything related to physical damage. She listened to Him and prayed. My body, mind, and heart were made completely new again.

I knew later that night that I was totally well because I noticed physical changes. I had no pain where I had physical pain for over thirty years. I had stacks of medical dictations declaring what was wrong in me. Now, I have stacks of papers documenting His healing and wholeness in me as I have complete healing and restoration in my body. I never knew life without severe abdominal pain, constant suicidal ideation/depression, aggressive treatments for pain, and various dosages of different medications for depression and pain. I also had an intestinal tract containing a football-size mass with complete nerve damage on the left side. The mass is totally gone. My intestinal tract is completely functioning. I have feeling on the left side of my intestines that I never had there before. He healed all the enemy's attempts to destroy my body through trauma and abuse.

My mind and heart have joy I've never experienced before. All my depression is completely gone. I have no more physical pain. I am no longer on any medications. Since then, my body has been functioning completely differently. I am learning what my new physical, emotional, and mental normal is. It's the life I only dreamed of. He came to make it a reality in me.

As though that didn't change my life forever in itself, she also led me through simple prayers of acknowledging the pain from my abusers and choosing to forgive them. I asked God to remove their sin, separate their sin from me, forgive and place their sins upon the cross, never to be held against them again. It was nothing complicated. No fancy prayers. They were prayers I had never prayed but were necessary for complete wholeness and healing for me. (Specific prayers of forgiveness/healing are found in her book *Power to Heal*.) I prayed to forgive all those who had hurt me and for everything they had done. Immediately, He healed the shattered remnants of my mind. I had yet to discover how my life would be so different.

Nights are no longer the same. I have a sound mind if I happen to wake in the middle of the night. I no longer wake in fear. Days are different. My mind is no longer confused, but quieted in His love and truth. I knew the enemy was upset that I was now completely free. I knew the days following my freedom were crucial in how my heart responded to normal daily events. I knew the way I used time now must be intensely intentional as my mind and heart had been cleansed from all darkness, sin, and bondage.

When freedom came, my Deliverer was calling me to be extremely diligent in what went into my mind and intentional as to how I chose to spend time. My mind was vulnerable to the open spaces the enemy left. I knew the Lord wanted to saturate and fill my mind with His absolute truth. Praise the Lord; He had already started this process in me as my desire for His truth increased the more I was healed.

I had no idea how much bondage I was in until I was set free! I immediately noticed a drastic hunger for Scriptures, His truth, and wanted to be with Him daily with increased understanding of His love and hope for me. I noticed how sensitive my spirit was to words I spoke as well as what others around me spoke. They weren't horrible conversations being heard, but caught my heart as being critical and tempting my heart to succumb to talk that was trivial and not uplifting. Often conversations were cutting toward others. They were directly against what truth teaches to remain in Him and to walk in freedom, so I left many conversations I would have normally engaged in, not thinking anything of them.

Many times throughout the next few days specifically, I recognized being intentional about what I listened to. I spend my time very differently now. I realized my mind and heart were a sponge the enemy would have loved to grab hold of again.

In order to keep the freedom the Lord had for me, I became diligent about guarding my heart and mind, regardless of what others' standards were in various areas. I couldn't watch the same television programs. I couldn't go to the same places. I couldn't have the same conversations without noticing common lies and distortions about who I believed I was.

Now I believed I was a daughter of the Most High God. I couldn't see myself the same way I saw myself before. I loved myself as God loves me. My perspectives about who I was were totally transformed. I knew I was loved, cherished, and treasured by Him. No longer could I talk about myself in a negative manner or cut myself down in conversations. I knew my talk about myself and others needed to change. I learned to reflect truth as I chose to discipline my mouth.

I couldn't listen to the normal talk I used to; I even noticed I had to filter my own thoughts. It was easy to walk in lies and have no idea. The enemy longs for us to be completely bombarded by lies so we will have no idea how they ensnare us and keep us in bondage. I began to aggressively monitor my thoughts like never before. As I cut out what was feeding lies in my life, the process of focusing, meditating, and choosing truth was easier.

Often words would be spoken to me that would not line up with truth about what God speaks over me. For example, when people were frustrated and spoke words not lining up with truth to me, I learned to cut off their words and curses spoken over me immediately after I was removed from the conversation. In the middle of the conversation, He taught me to not receive those words and curses in my spirit. When we don't have lies, strongholds, or darkness for the enemy to attach to, he cannot gain ground unless we receive those words spoken. This was a huge revelation to me. I was amazed how words spoken can have tremendous power. We do not have to receive words that do not line up with the Word of God. We have authority in Christ to break off every word curse and lie spoken over us in Jesus' name. In place of word curses, we need to fill those vulnerable places with His truth.

This became more evident to me the more I recognized how sneaky the enemy is in trying to deter me from my freedom. The enemy doesn't come to us in a red suit and pitchfork, but attempts to convince us in our minds with thoughts directly from him. Thoughts such as *I will never be free or walk in all the Lord has for me* are a direct lie from the enemy. Satan is subtle, as his goal is for believers to never recognize his attempts to destroy us. Once we recognize who our enemy is, we can fight directly against him with truth. The truth is the Lord came to set all of us free! The truth is the Lord desires for us to walk out every amazing plan He has for us and fulfill all of our destinies in Him.

I no longer live in pain, horror, grief, or torment. After years of the horror and torment experienced in Satanic Ritual Abuse, I am ecstatic to tell you that God has healed me from every night of terror. He makes my nights times of true rest and causes me to lie down in safety. My heart is no longer afraid to lie down. My soul is ministered to in His dreams over me during the night. My ears no longer hear screaming and crying from rituals. Instead, my ears hear the living God singing over me, warring over me, and interceding on my behalf. He healed every horrific memory and restored those graphic places of trauma in my mind with vivid pictures of His grace and mercy. He gives me pictures to color to Him as my response of worship. The memories related to darkness have been replaced by His times of rescuing me out of those pits. They are now pictures of how amazing and loving I know Him to be. They are pictures of truth, joy and life only expressed through worship and the colors He lets me paint.

He has rescued and redeemed my life from the pit of darkness and brought this soul into His light, a glorious light that only He can create. My greatest delight is to worship the Lord and dance before Him filled with praise to Him for all He has done in me. He is the only One who is worthy to be praised.

Never did I imagine my life would be healed. I was hoping for relief and soothing from pain, but I didn't know total transformation of my heart and mind would ever be reality. Only by His unbelievable grace and mercy am I able to declare how amazing God is. I am not only sane, but also no longer broken in my mind. I think clearly and hear only my thoughts and the voice of the Holy Spirit or the enemy. This is a huge difference when I was used to hearing a chorus and a roar of voices inside my head, 24/7, ever since I can remember.

Now, because my mind is quiet, and alters have integrated, I am able to live my life and finish the tasks I have every day. I never thought this would be possible. I am able to sleep through the nights now. They are filled with prayers of intercession for those still in bondage. They are filled with praise and worship to the One who is worthy. If I awake during the night, I often pray for those the Lord is still rescuing. I meditate on Him and His truth now and listen to Him.

I can think clearly now. Simple tasks of going to the grocery store and picking up milk and eggs used to be quite a dramatic adventure, getting many more items the ones inside would demand. Before, I would walk out of the store two hours later without the receipt to keep track of what I had purchased. My bank account would have turned to rubber and bounced. But now, I can think clearly with no interruptions of alters and can decide to go to the store to get milk and eggs, and it's all I purchase. I walk away with a receipt to budget with. It's a totally different experience. It's so peaceful knowing where the hours go because I no longer lose time. However, I will still probably have a variety of clocks at home, just to be sure!

I now go places and am present as myself the whole time. It has made an incredible difference to be in a church service, mentally present as myself the whole service and no longer triggered like I used to be. I no longer run out of the church when crosses are displayed. When communion plates are passed to me, I no longer throw the container of miniature cups of grape juice and plate of bread in fear. They no longer land in the pew in front of me, causing quite a disturbance and an interruption in how that plate was going to get to the rest of the people.

I no longer shout profanities when worship includes songs about the blood of Christ and His love for us. It is totally different now. My eyes fill with tears even as I think about His healing in me from all these areas. The enemy wanted so badly for me to never see the truth of Christ. The enemy didn't want me to know the significance of Christ's blood and His work on the cross. The enemy has been crushed under my feet, and he just got exposed. Christ is triumphant over all the schemes of hell.

The Lord's purposes for my life will prevail, and His truth will be revealed to me and continue to set me free as I cling to Christ. Never again will I turn from the cross of Christ, since I now know the true significance. The enemy didn't want me to have any idea how powerful Christ's work on the cross was. Satan tried to distort and pervert the cross in every way he could in the satanic ceremonies I was forced to be a part of. No longer will the cross and work of Christ be perverted in my mind and my heart! Praise be to God.

I embrace the cross like nothing else in life. The cross has literally become the crux of my entire freedom and wholeness. The sacrifice Jesus Christ made on the cross as His payment for my sin and the horror is inextricably linked to my entire life of freedom. He made a way for me. He made a way of life and joy because of His sacrifice of love for me. His truth concerning His cross is no longer distorted in my mind. Instead, it represents the pure, selfless love He has for me. He expects nothing in return. My heart's response, however, is to love Him with all I am.

He loved me this way before I could ever respond to Him. He loves me no matter what choices I will ever make in life. His love for me will never change. His love for me will always be more than I can handle, because I am but dust created to grasp whatever He allows in His mercy. His mercy has His love continually overtaking and overwhelming my heart. I will never find the end of His love for me. He will surprise me with waves and floods of His love for me for the rest of my days.

As I have discovered this kind of love in His freeing work in my life, there is no other response I have to Him but worship. My days are filled with new pictures of praise to be brought before Him and new dances to tap to Him in my dreams. Being free and whole is a new life He has given me. My best attempts to reveal what He has done in me are expressed in my worship to Him. My words often don't bring justice to my heart's gratitude for what He has done in me. But He now gives me words. Where I was afraid of my voice for speaking out, He has given me a voice to shout jubilations and exaltations before Him.

He took my fear away. He gave me faith to rise to my destiny and proclaim liberty for the captives and healing for the broken. He gave me gifts to walk His purposes out in my life. I have opened them. Two of them are especially significant. Among His fancy ribbons and wrapping paper is a new journal, to hold His continued work in my life, and a new red pen to keep scribing the wonders of who He is and what He has done.

My heart is whole now. I hear Him and He says He loves me far beyond my understanding and comprehension. I see Him and He dances with feet of paintbrushes sweeping colors on canvases He calls my destiny. I feel Him and He holds me in Him arms and keeps me safe from darkness. He breathes life over me and speaks affirmations of love for me. I smell Him. The fragrance He makes for me takes me in fields where I now run and play and laugh and dance the freedom He has given me. I know Him now. He is my Deliverer, Savior, and Healer. He is also my Father, my Papa, words I didn't imagine ever calling Him, but now do.

Shortly after I was healed I couldn't help but proclaim what He had done in me. I had shared with several immediately about what took place and how He healed me. Some knew my journey for years, while others didn't know me aside from work or seeing them in stores. I couldn't help but share what had happened to me with a woman who didn't know the Lord. I shared with her how I knew everything was different. She continued to ask questions as I shared with her.

I wrote her a letter on the train telling how God healed me from all my pain and took my trauma away. I told how He set my heart free and that my mind and heart weren't shattered anymore from all the abuse I had known. It was a simple letter that I couldn't seem to write fast enough to tell her what He did and how amazing He was. I told her He could heal all of the hurts in her life also if she wanted Him to, and He wanted her to know Him. After she read the letter she accepted the Lord and His healing for her life also. I knew at that point my healing wasn't just so I could be free, but also so I could proclaim from the rooftops, or train, or aisle in the store, or flying on a plane across the seas that He alone has come to heal and liberate us.

My soul has many songs inside: songs of praise and worship to the King of kings. My mind has a new voice. This one He has given me to declare and shout forth praise to the One who set me free. My voice will now proclaim freedom and healing to those captive.

Questions to Consider

1. How have you come to know Him as your Redeemer?

2. How have you come to know Him as your Healer?

3. How have you come to know Him as your Deliverer?

4. How has He highlighted Himself in your heart as you have read these chapters?

5. How has He ministered to you through these chapters?

6. Read Isaiah 61. What is your place in His Kingdom Church?

7. How does the Lord desire to minister Isaiah 61 in you? In others?

ENCOURAGEMENT FOR THOSE HURTING AND THOSE WHO HELP

If you have gained nothing else from these pages, my prayer is for you to have gathered glimpses of Him who came to set us free. I pray you have seen the God of all hope. He gives strength to endure until complete freedom and healing are yours. I pray you persevere in pursuing your promised land of victory as you continue to walk out of your "Egypt." I pray these pages have caused you to grow hungry for the One who is capable and willing to completely fill and satisfy.

Let our goal be not only to rid ourselves of pain and rough roads, but to encounter Him. When we encounter His love, we also find Him as our Rescuer and our Savior. Let us know Him even more intimately for who He truly is. May we know Him in all His fullness, not merely for what He can do for us, but for Himself.

When we come to discover who He is, the freedom and healing longed for will come and often blindside us. When we least expect He often comes and makes Himself known to us in His extravagance. He comes in the specific ways we need. Our gaze is no longer on our own pain and what we desperately desire concerning healing, but it has turned.

When we lock eyes with the One who loves us with unfailing love, transformation and His change in us will inevitably take place, though we may not even be looking for it. The byproduct of healing becomes secondary to our newfound priority of Him alone. When we gain tenacious trust in Him and His character, greater measures of freedom occur. Paradigm shifts solidify when we seek Him and His truth on a steeper scale versus our persistence to be free of a painful past.

For those who encourage those hurting, I pray you were brought to increased understanding and increased love for Him who came for their freedom. As you're a companion to walking others out of captivity, I pray you were brought closer to His heart for the hurting as you carry one end of the "stretcher" to Jesus Christ.

CPSIA information can be obtained at www.ICGtesting.com
Printed in the USA
LVOW132027181212

312272LV00001B/135/P